NOT EXACTLY
ROCKET SCIENCE

FOR ELLA,
WITH BEST WISHES!

BRENT
COULSON

D1606904

NOT EXACTLY ROCKET SCIENCE

A COLLECTION OF CARTOONS BY
BRENT COULSON

SMiRK
Productions

NOT EXACTLY ROCKET SCIENCE

ISBN: 0-9665637-0-0

Library of Congress Catalog Card Number: 98-90529

*This book is dedicated to my family, my friends, and anyone else who has
ever had to put up with me asking, "Do you think this is funny?"*

Soccer ball practical jokes

After years of just "nipping," Jack Frost finally opened a clinic for nose jobs.

Corn flakes

"Sorry guys, my mom won't let me
play with matches."

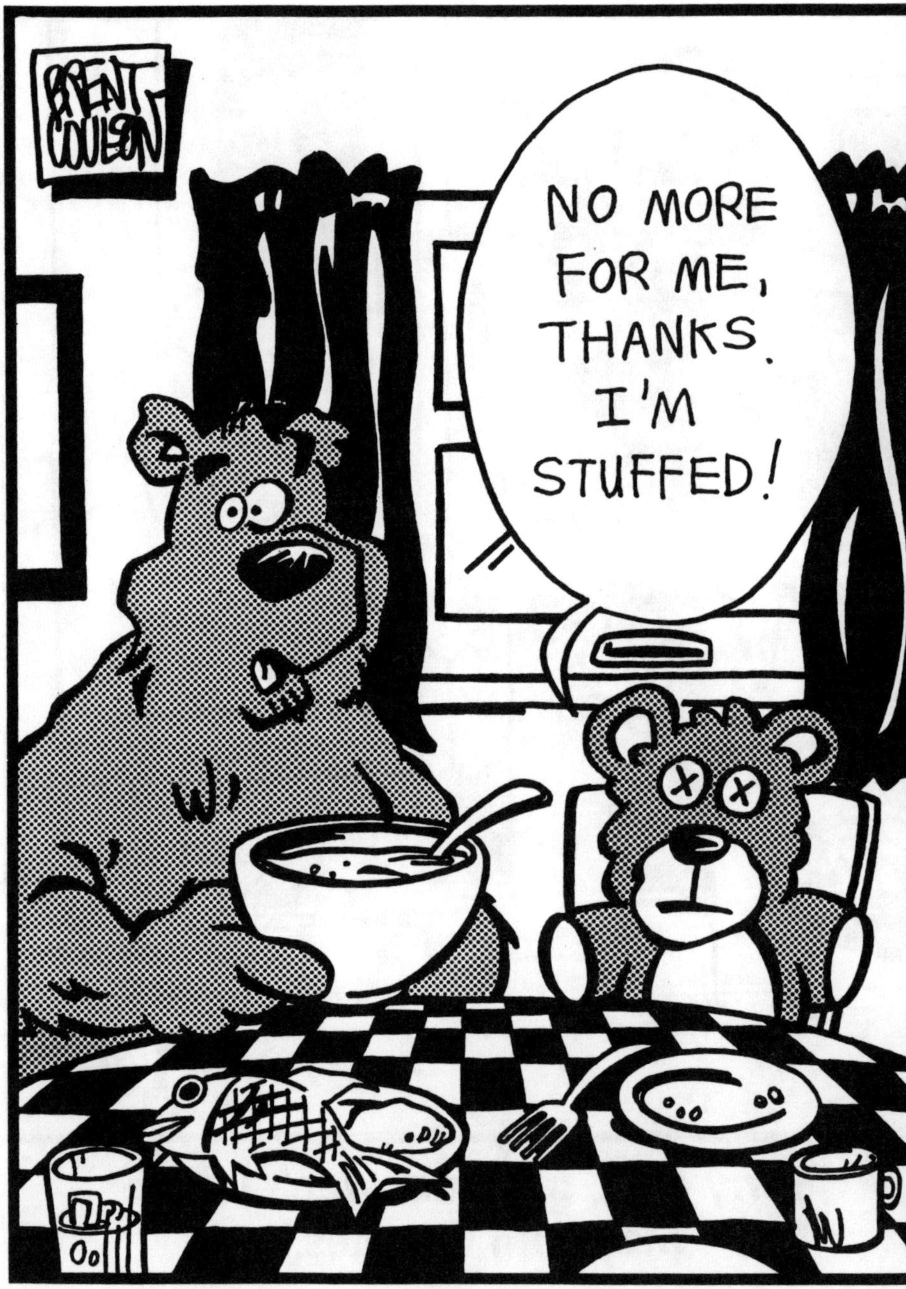
BRENT COULSON
NO MORE FOR ME, THANKS. I'M STUFFED!

**Dragons who can't breathe fire
have to use the microwave.**

"I'm sorry, but we're looking for someone with a little more 'Pop!' "

When mimes get arrested

Tarzan often had trouble getting into fast food restaurants.

When all of her children were grown
and she still didn't know what to do,
the little old lady who lived in a shoe
bought a mobile home.

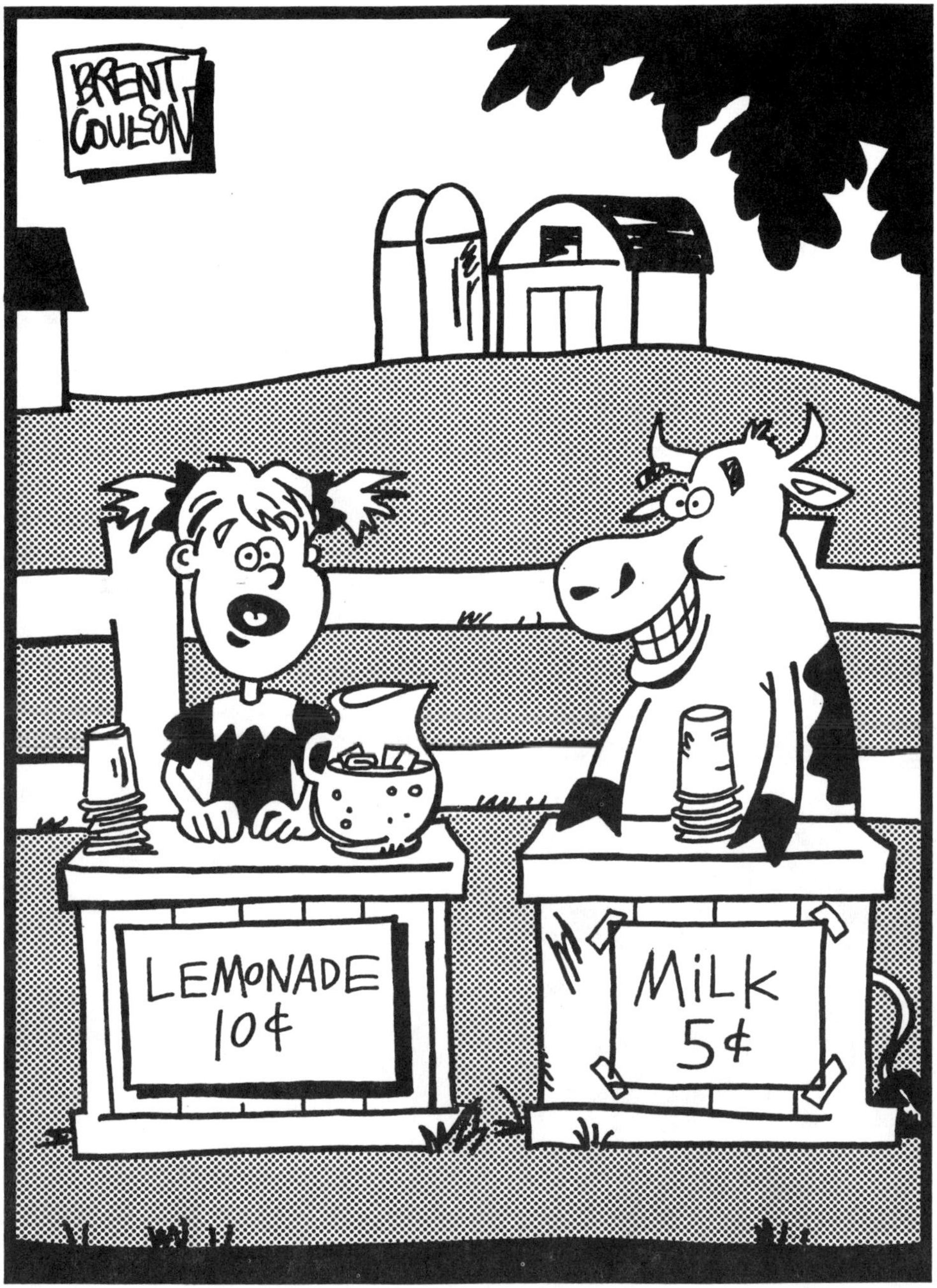
BRENT COULSON
LEMONADE
10¢
MiLK
5¢

Primitive history classes were often very informal.

"Yes Mr. Ahab, you are on our passenger list, but I can't let you on the boat with that harpoon."

"I told you this is *much* more exciting than the Stairmaster at the health club."

"If our jersey numbers really were our I.Q.'s,
I'd be…like, twice as smart as you."

When golf caddies become disgruntled

"Is it hot in here or is it just me?"

Of course in an actual emergency
situation, Jerry panicked.

"Okay then, tell me if it hurts
when I do this..."

**Dumbfounded by his good luck,
Cyclops couldn't believe his eye.**

21

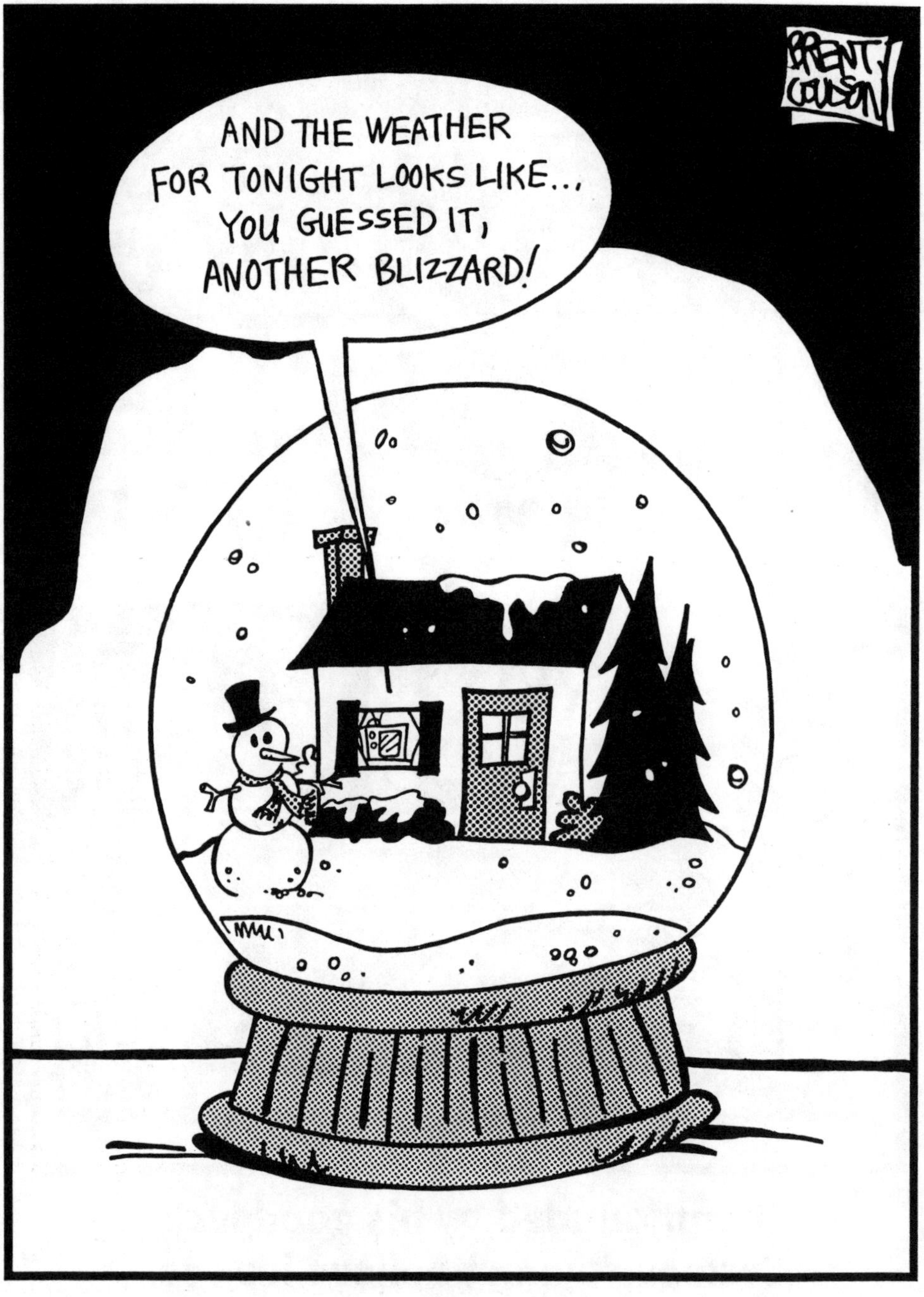
BRENT COULSON
AND THE WEATHER FOR TONIGHT LOOKS LIKE... YOU GUESSED IT, ANOTHER BLIZZARD!

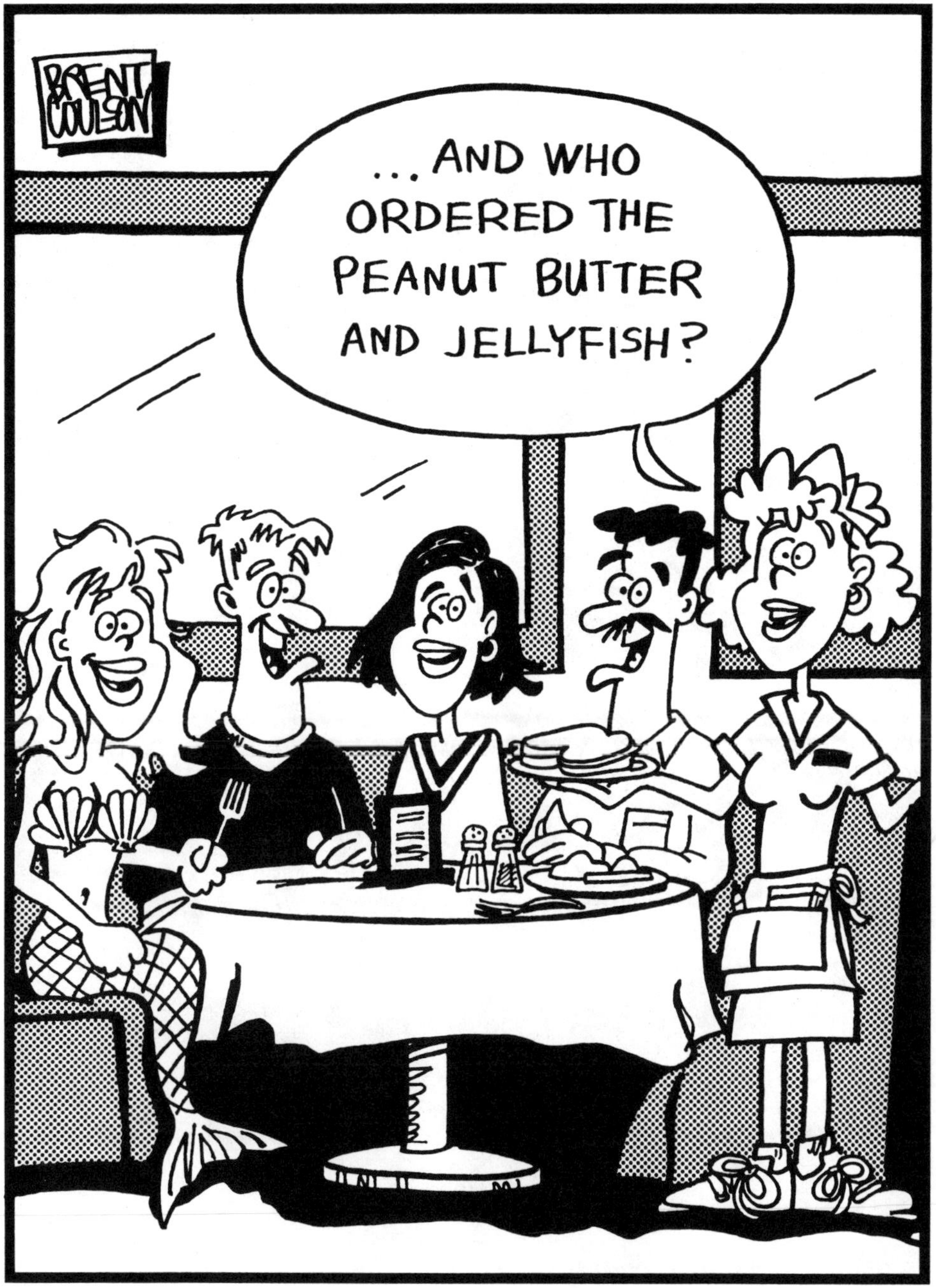
BRENT COULSON
...AND WHO ORDERED THE PEANUT BUTTER AND JELLYFISH?

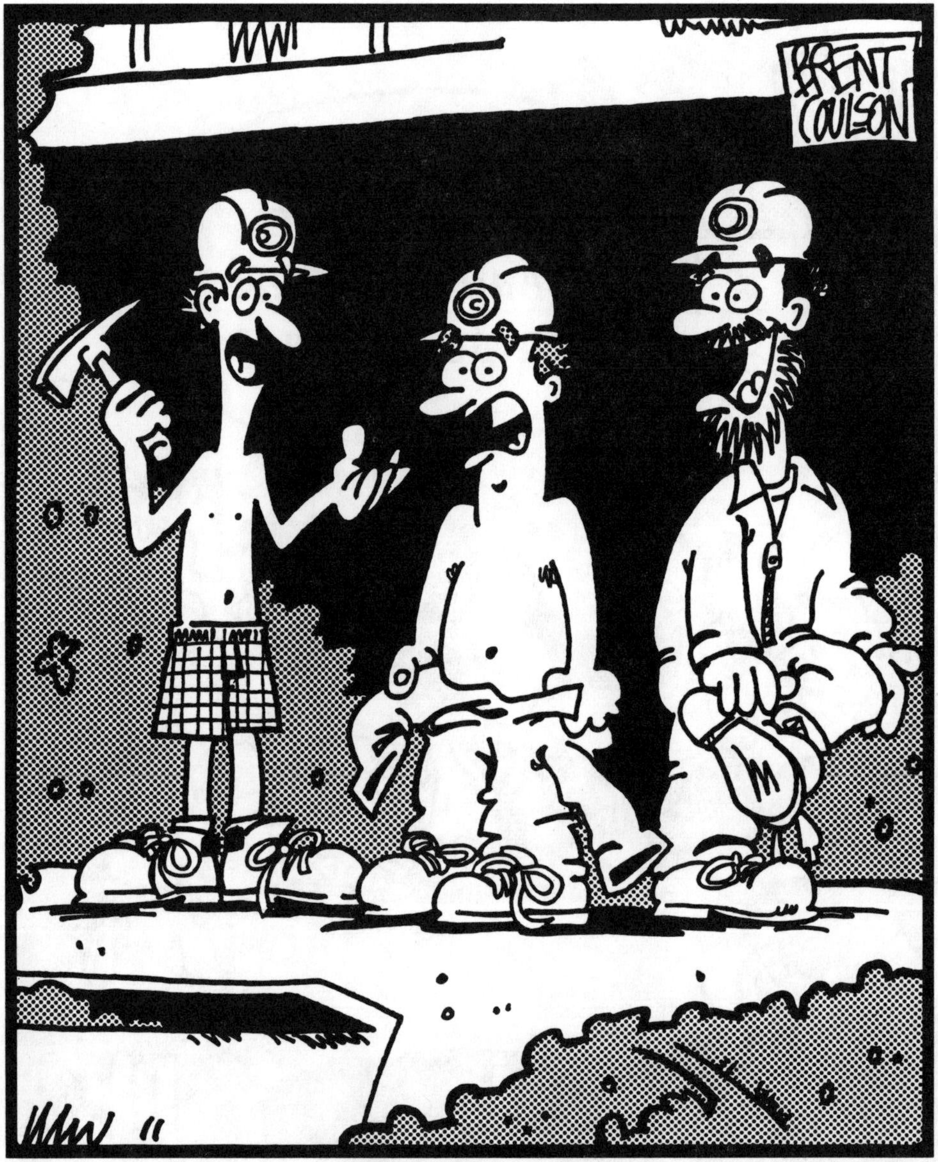
BRENT COULSON

Strip mining

Godzilla's bug spray

Although Charles Darwin's parents never understood his theory of evolution, they were still very proud of him.

**The case of Wile E. Coyote vs.
Acme Explosives, Inc.**

"Do you wanna make s'mores?"

26

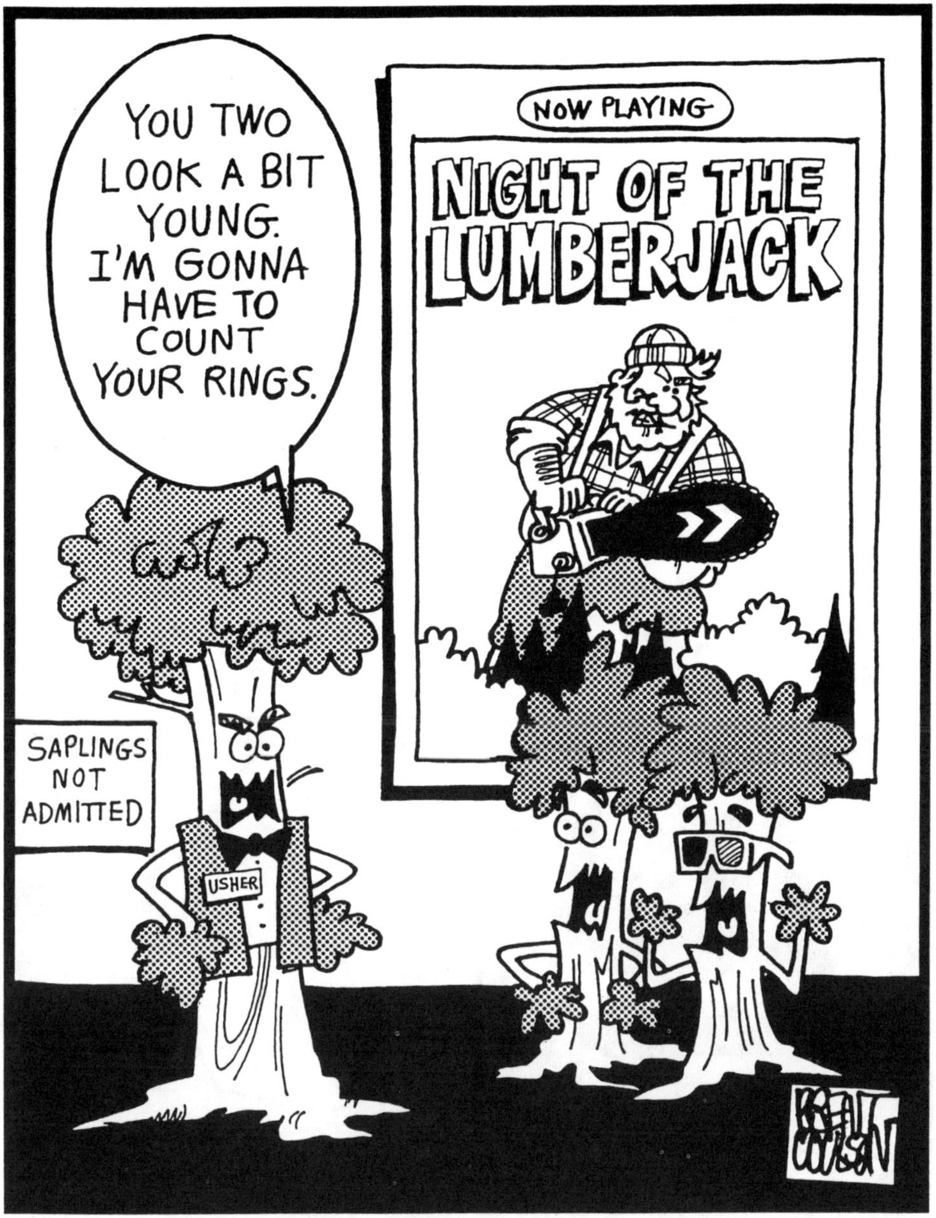
YOU TWO LOOK A BIT YOUNG. I'M GONNA HAVE TO COUNT YOUR RINGS.
NOW PLAYING
NIGHT OF THE LUMBERJACK
SAPLINGS NOT ADMITTED
USHER

Tree horror movies

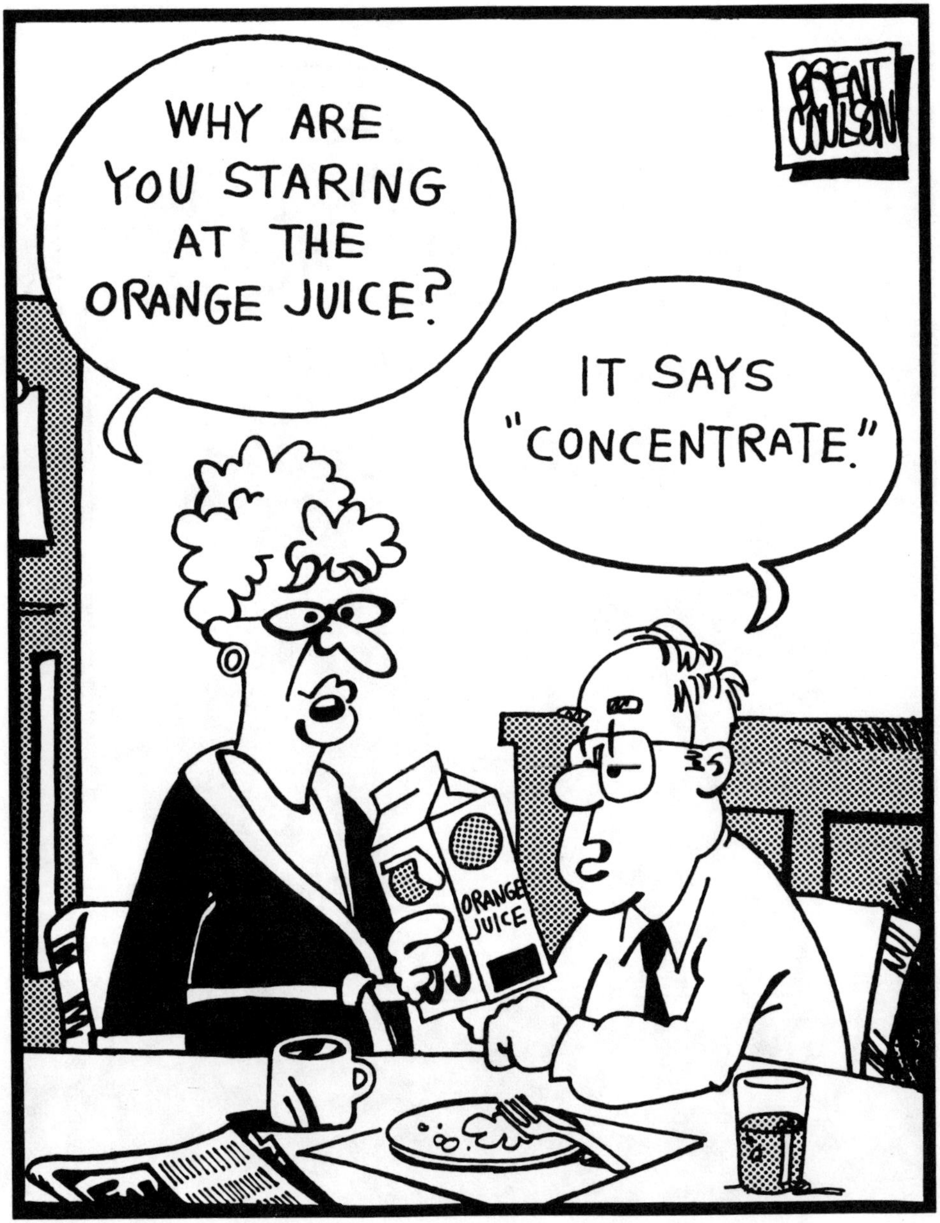
WHY ARE YOU STARING AT THE ORANGE JUICE?
IT SAYS "CONCENTRATE."
ORANGE JUICE
BRENT COULSON

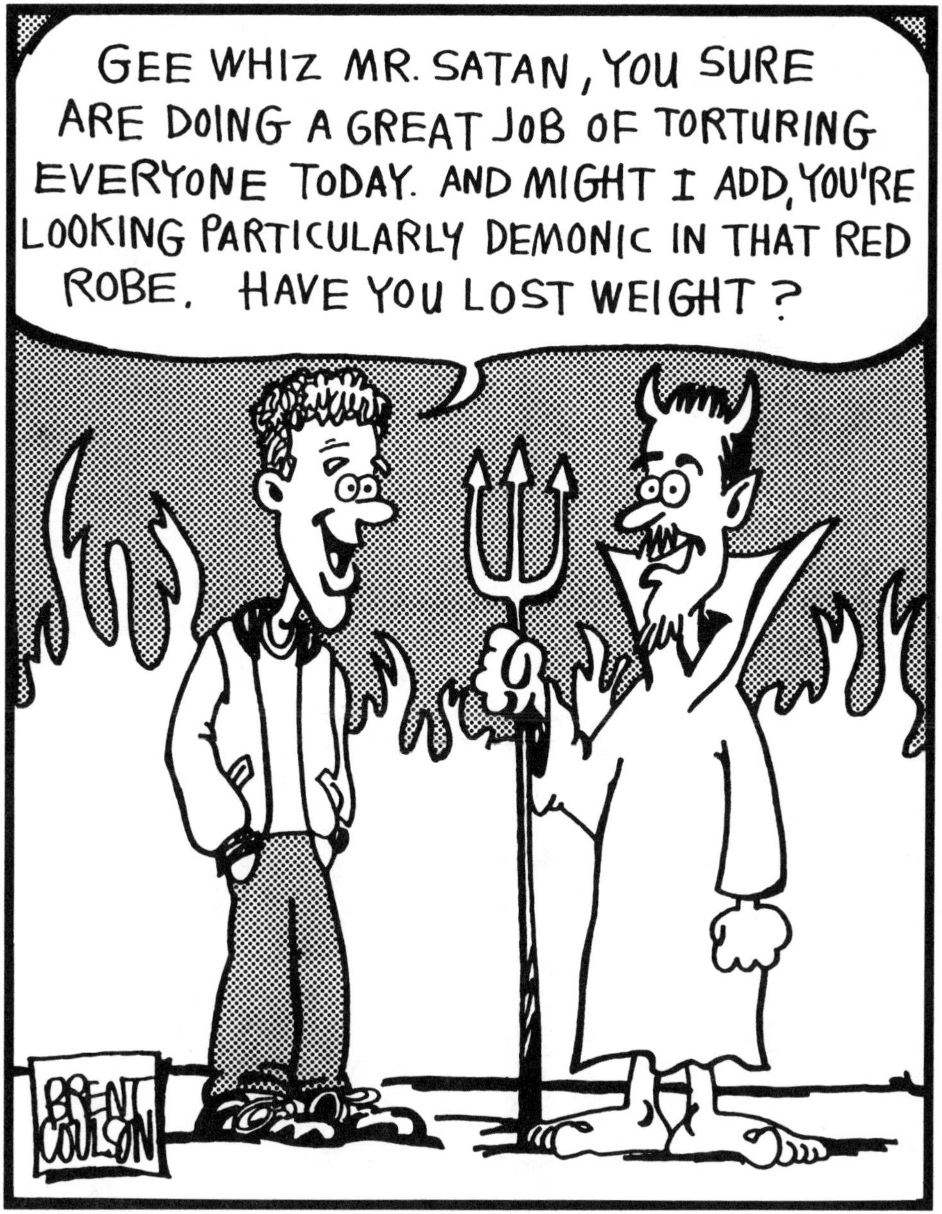
GEE WHIZ MR. SATAN, YOU SURE ARE DOING A GREAT JOB OF TORTURING EVERYONE TODAY. AND MIGHT I ADD, YOU'RE LOOKING PARTICULARLY DEMONIC IN THAT RED ROBE. HAVE YOU LOST WEIGHT?
BRENT COULSON

Eddie Haskell in Hell

Paul Revere in the first grade

Open heart surgery on the Tin Man

"I'm sorry Og, but this relationship just isn't evolving the way I thought it would."

Sigmund Fraud

"Nevermind. I thought I had found two snowflakes that were identical, but the one on the left is dandruff."

The Leader of the Pachyderms

The Wright brothers had a younger brother Icarus, who never received any credit for his contributions to the invention of the airplane.

"I'm sorry Roy, but I had to let him sit up front. He called 'Shotgun' right after I cuffed him."

35

**Geppetto grew much lonelier
after Pinocchio left him.**

36

"Why no, we don't have a dental plan.
Why do you ask?"

3-D horror films for small mammals

Disc jockeys

"You'd better make the next one
a double. I'm not even buzzing yet!"

39

Moses as a boy

"That's not our flock. That's just a bunch of M's!
Boy, this is sure going to be embarrassing."

"I'm still not sure. Could you have
number two step forward again?"

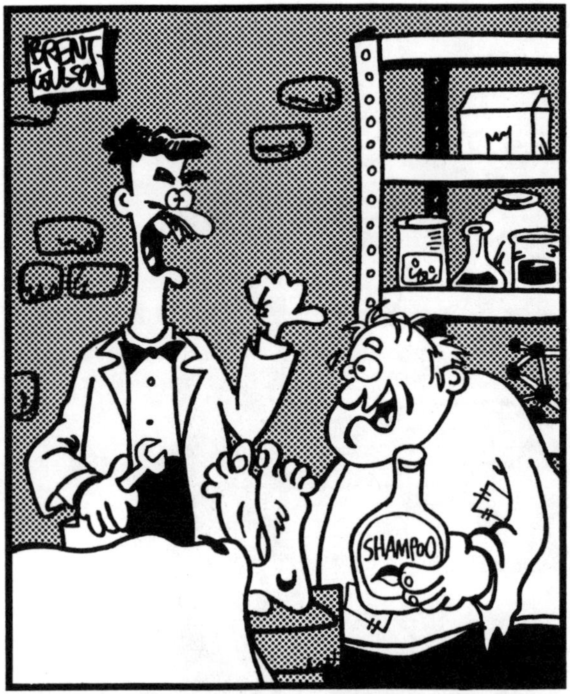
BRENT COULSON
SHAMPOO

"Nobody likes a smart aleck hunchback, Igor. Now go get me *the monster's* head and shoulders!"

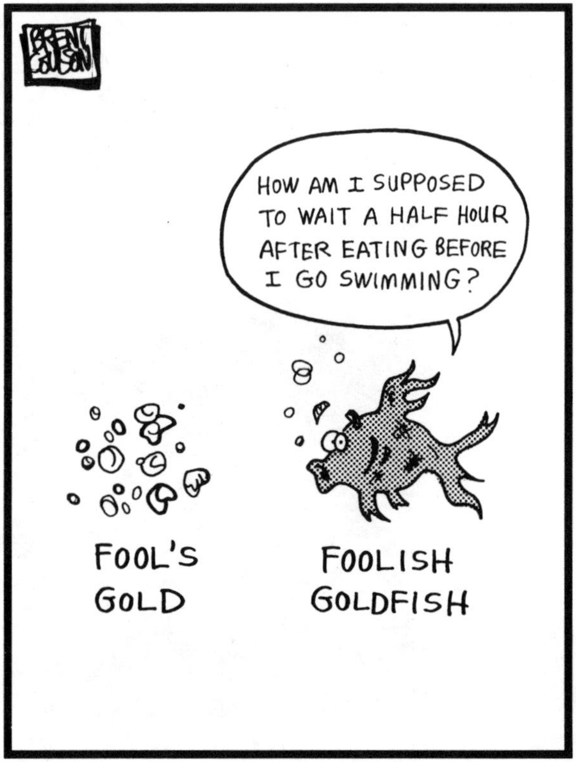
BRENT COULSON
HOW AM I SUPPOSED TO WAIT A HALF HOUR AFTER EATING BEFORE I GO SWIMMING?
FOOL'S GOLD
FOOLISH GOLDFISH

Noah got a little careless with the unicorn.

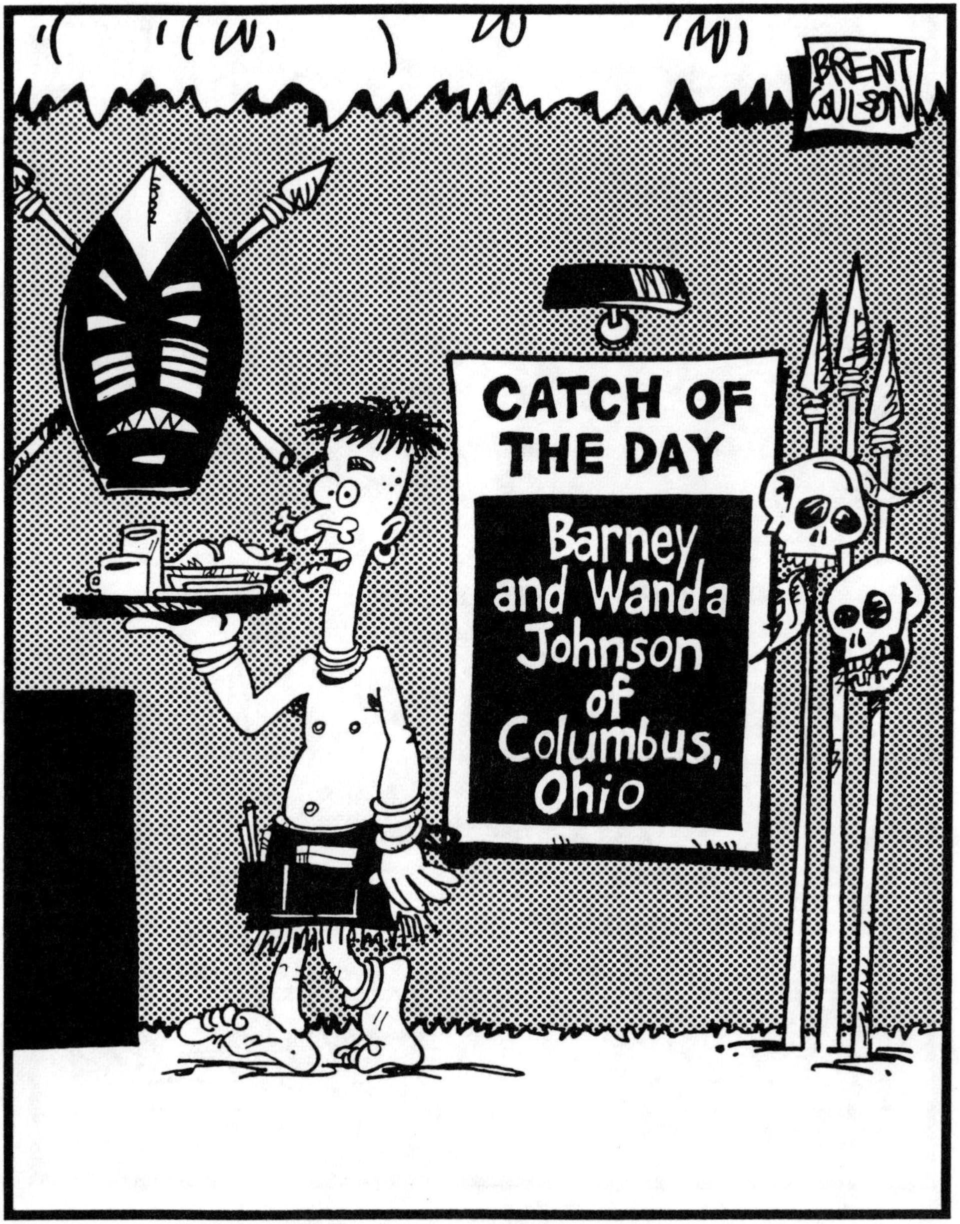
BRENT COULSON
CATCH OF THE DAY
Barney and Wanda Johnson of Columbus, Ohio

The Cannibal Café

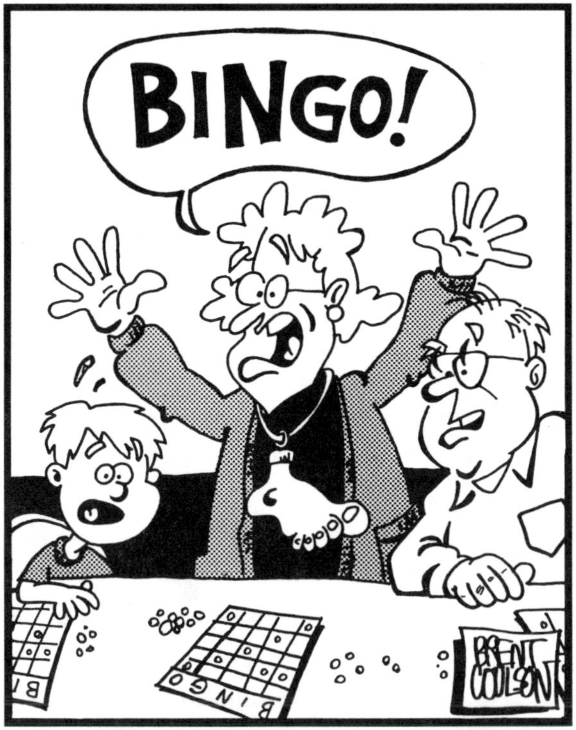
BINGO!
BRENT COULSON

Although they were playing in the basement of a Lutheran church, Betsy and her lucky rabbi's foot were unbeatable.

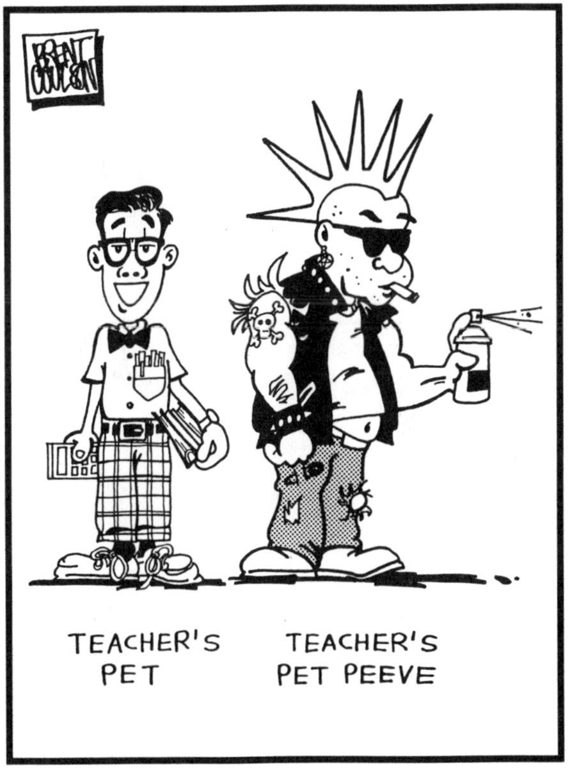
BRENT COULSON
TEACHER'S PET
TEACHER'S PET PEEVE

**"Maybe you misunderstood me, Doc.
The shingles are out in my truck.
I'm here to fix your roof!"**

"Boy, I just can't tell you how many times
this stuff has saved me from muggers."

**Contrary to popular belief,
Captain Hook's nickname actually came
from his high school basketball days.**

College-ruled zebra

"Oh no! Not *this clown* again!"

Stephen was a real snake charmer

"Lady, that sign is the route number, not the speed limit!"

Jaws as a teenager

When skunk children are missing

Conan the Barber

Ultimately, Ben lost his job as a shepherd because he fell asleep every time he tried to count his sheep.

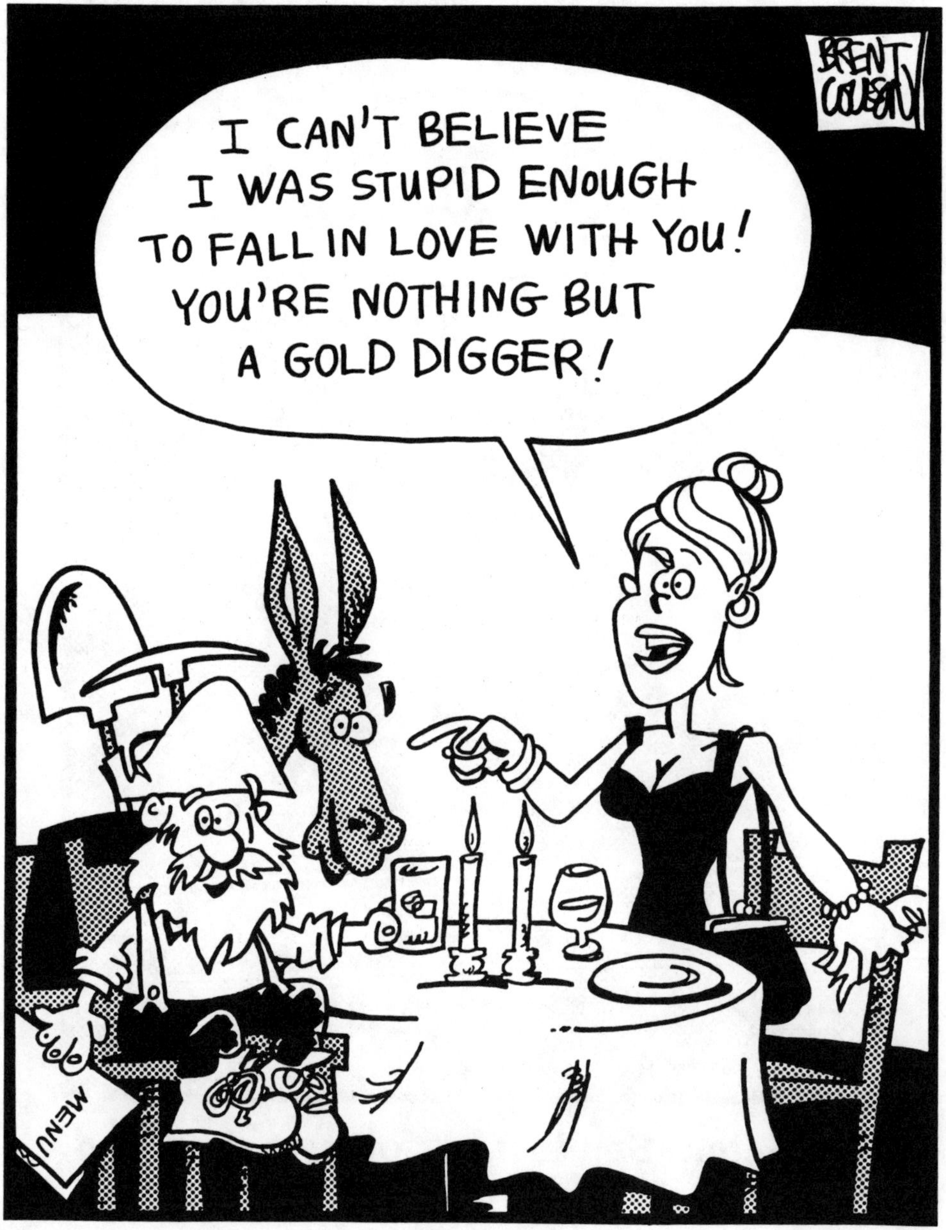
BRENT COUSEN
I CAN'T BELIEVE I WAS STUPID ENOUGH TO FALL IN LOVE WITH YOU! YOU'RE NOTHING BUT A GOLD DIGGER!
MENU

When vampires argue

George Washington's dentist

Tyrannosaurus wrecks

Matchbook unions

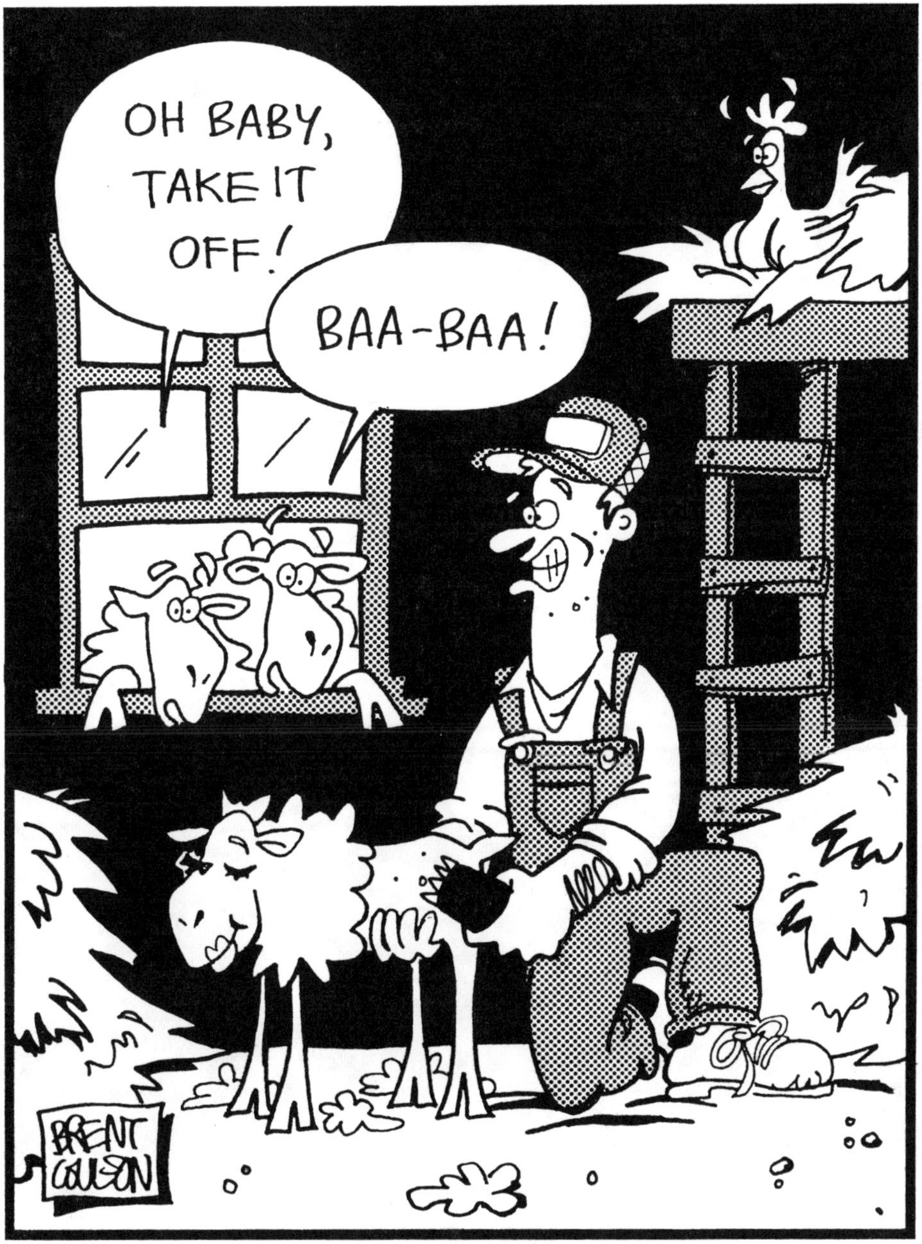
OH BABY, TAKE IT OFF!
BAA-BAA!
BRENT COULSON

Little Bo Peep Shows

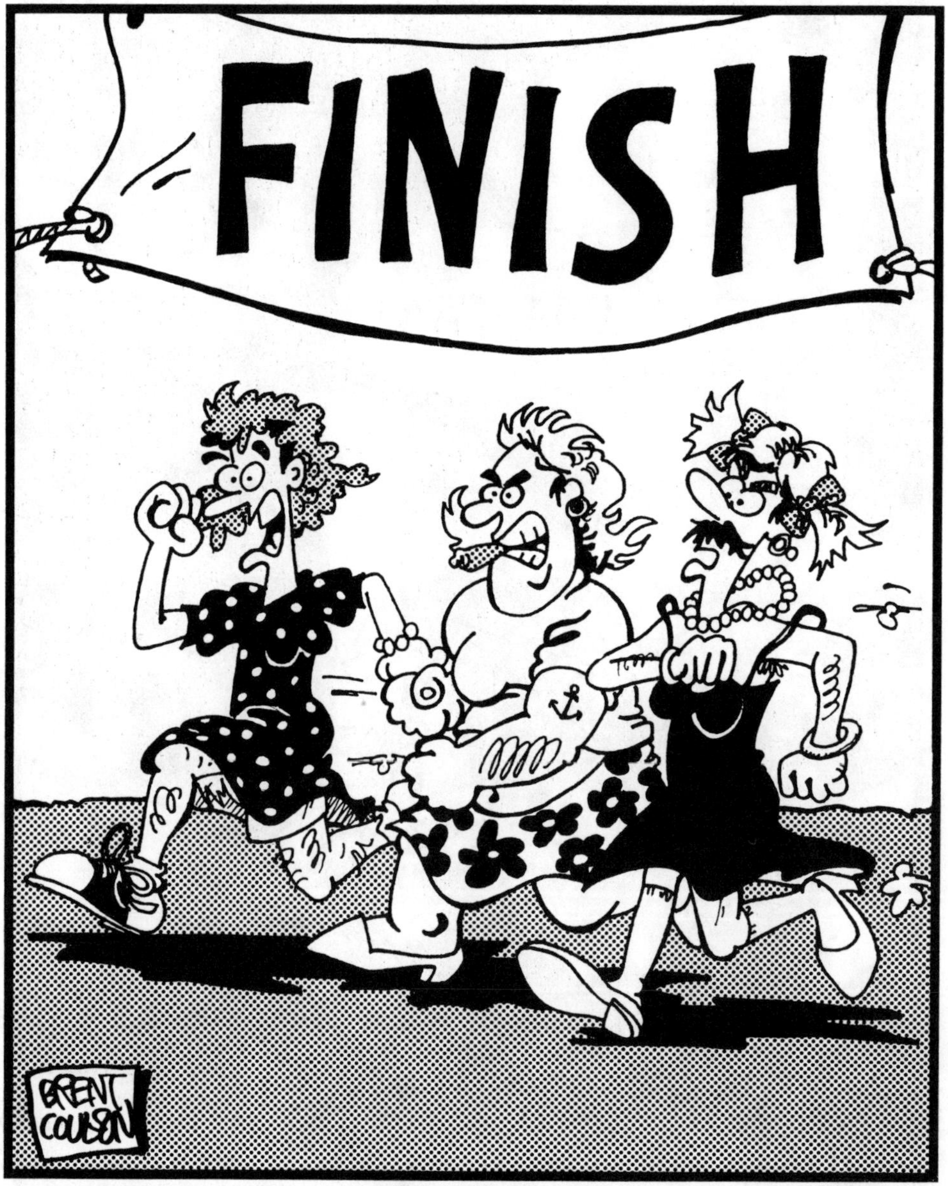
FINISH
BRENT COULSON

Drag races

John Paul, George and Ringo

"You know I never really believed in the tooth fairy, but this morning my dentures were gone, and there was $200 under my pillow."

On the first day of Roger's summer job,
he went to the wrong place.

**Mr. Peanut vs.
George Washington Carver**

Forrest Grump

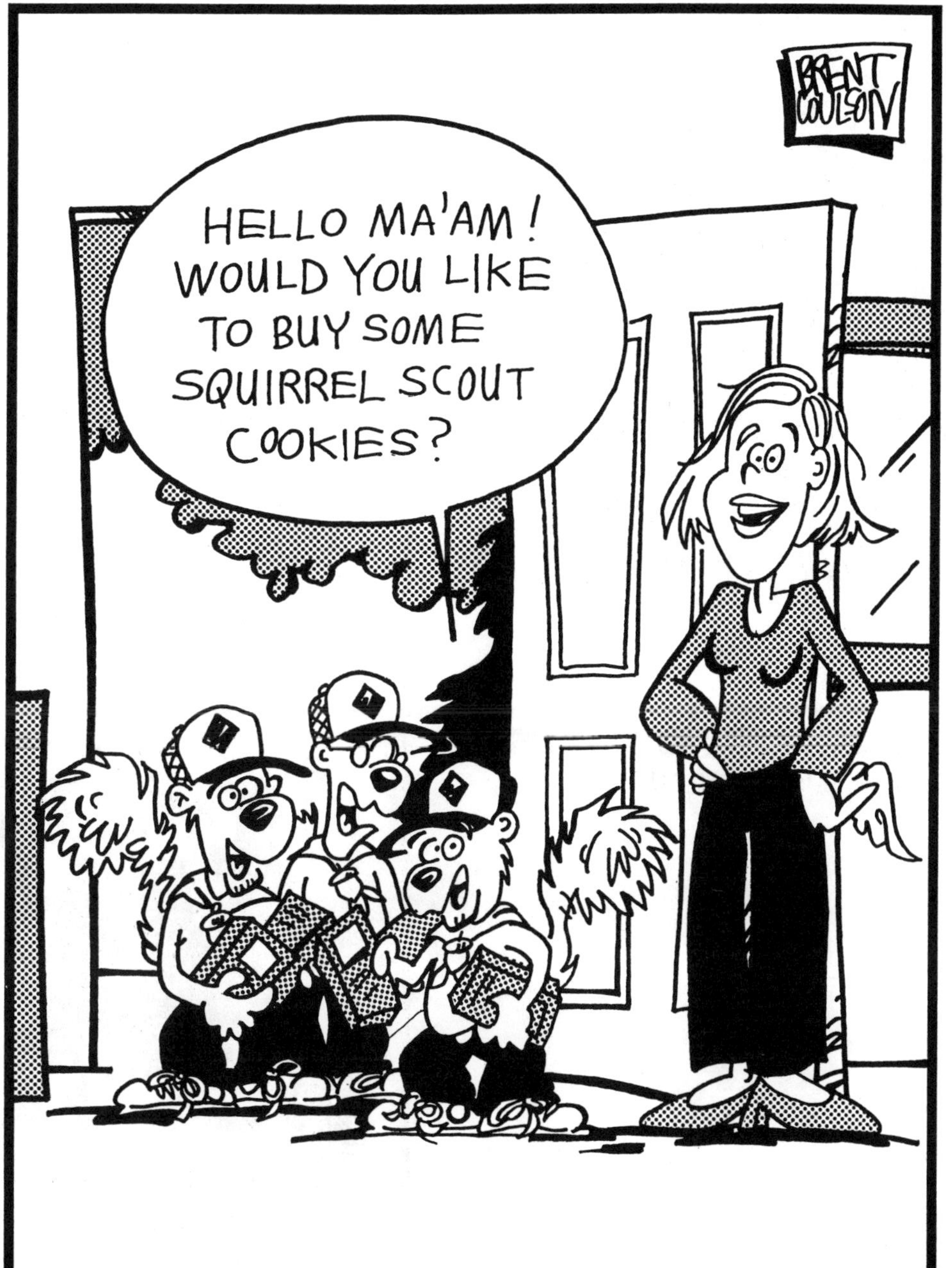
BRENT COULSON
HELLO MA'AM! WOULD YOU LIKE TO BUY SOME SQUIRREL SCOUT COOKIES?

"Uh-oh! Brussels sprouts?!?"

Mother Inferior

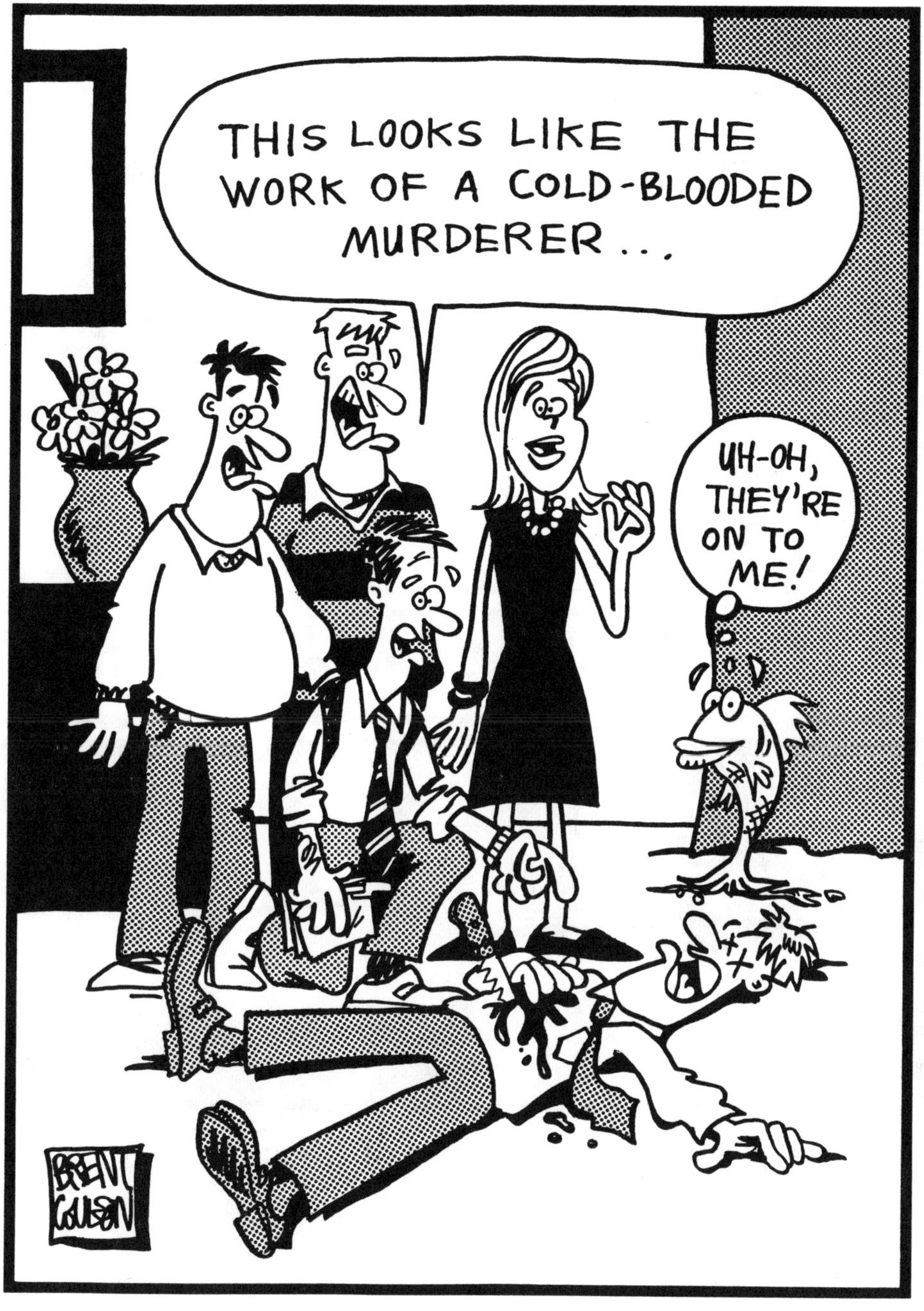
THIS LOOKS LIKE THE WORK OF A COLD-BLOODED MURDERER...
UH-OH, THEY'RE ON TO ME!
BRENT COULSON

**Edith sensed that the postal workers
were feeling a bit disgruntled today.**

"When I said you should wear pumps
with that dress, that's not exactly
what I had in mind."

Bert's bum knee kept acting up

"Hey Doug, check out this view! Times like this make you feel like you could live forever."

"No way Romulus! It's your turn.
I took Mom for a walk last time!"

Superheroes who never made it big

Seymour was really sad when his dog ran away.

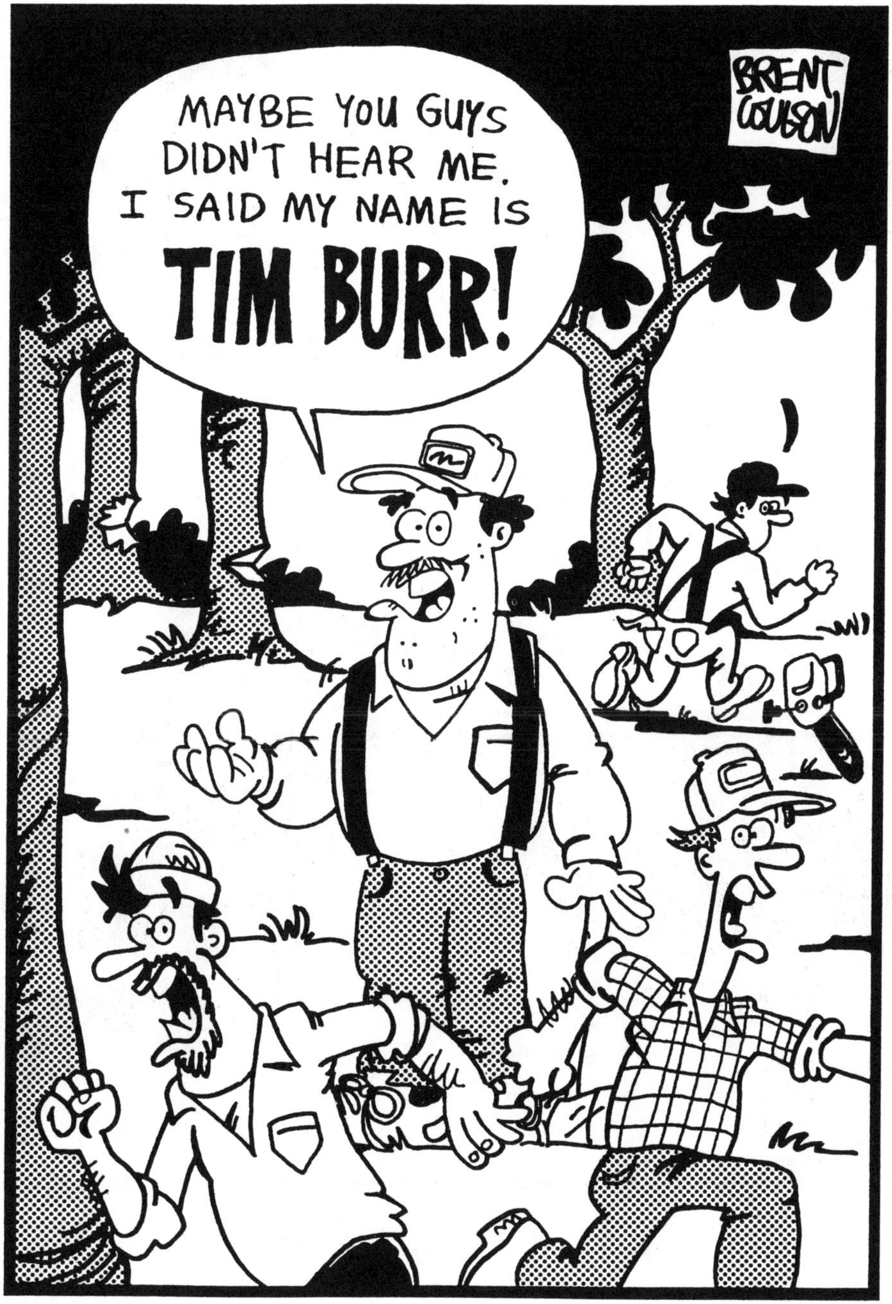
BRENT COULSON
MAYBE YOU GUYS DIDN'T HEAR ME. I SAID MY NAME IS TIM BURR!

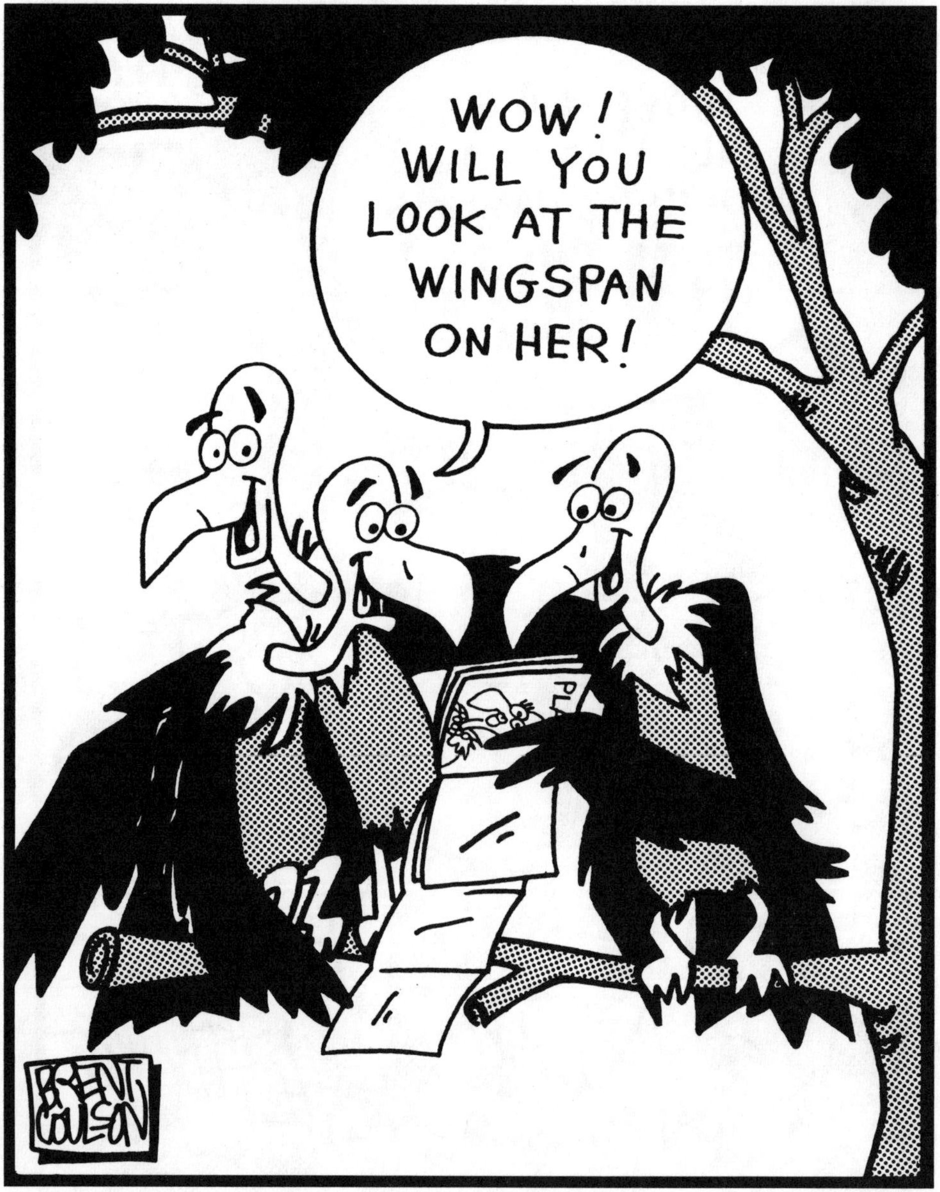
WOW! WILL YOU LOOK AT THE WINGSPAN ON HER!
BRENT COULSON

Condor centerfolds

Pinocchio always had trouble using a fake I.D.

When worms go fishing

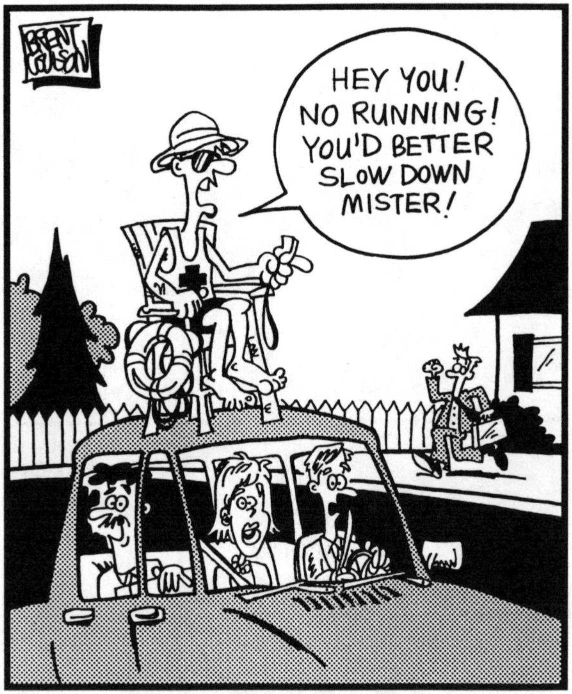
BRENT COULSON
HEY YOU! NO RUNNING! YOU'D BETTER SLOW DOWN MISTER!

Carpool lifeguard

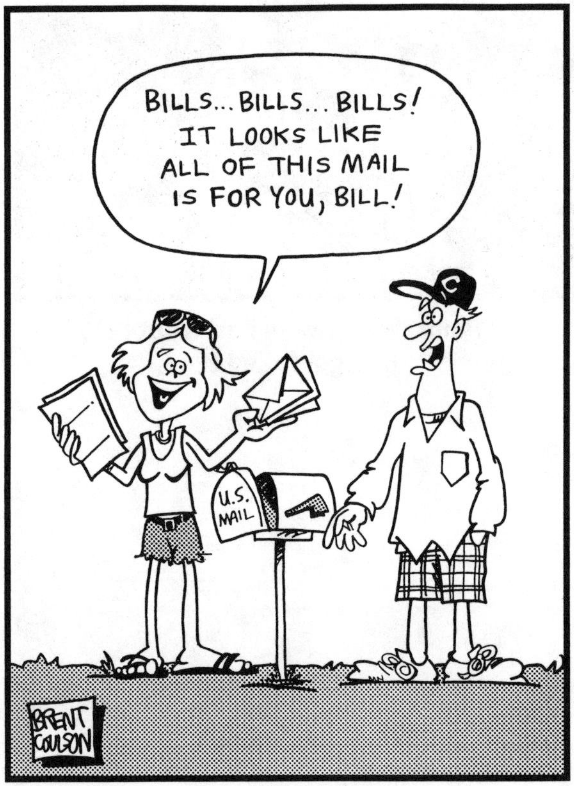
BILLS... BILLS... BILLS! IT LOOKS LIKE ALL OF THIS MAIL IS FOR YOU, BILL!
U.S. MAIL
BRENT COULSON

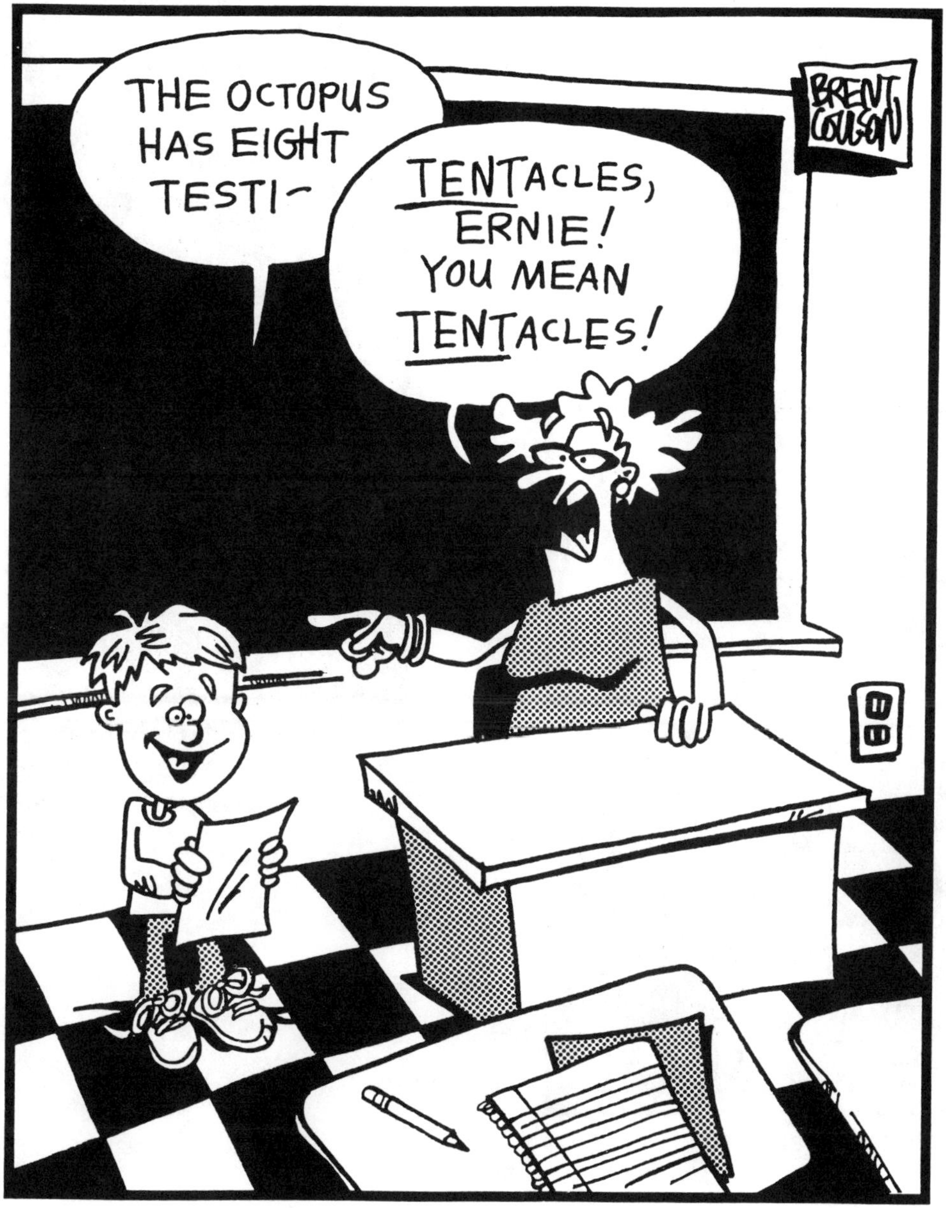
THE OCTOPUS HAS EIGHT TESTI-
TENTACLES, ERNIE! YOU MEAN TENTACLES!
BRENT COULSON

Laboratory retrievers

Although Captain Spatula was not as famous as Captain Hook, he was much more fun at cookouts.

"Oh, for crying out loud! Bobby, give him
some of your dog food and maybe
he'll stop begging."

Cemetery work schedules

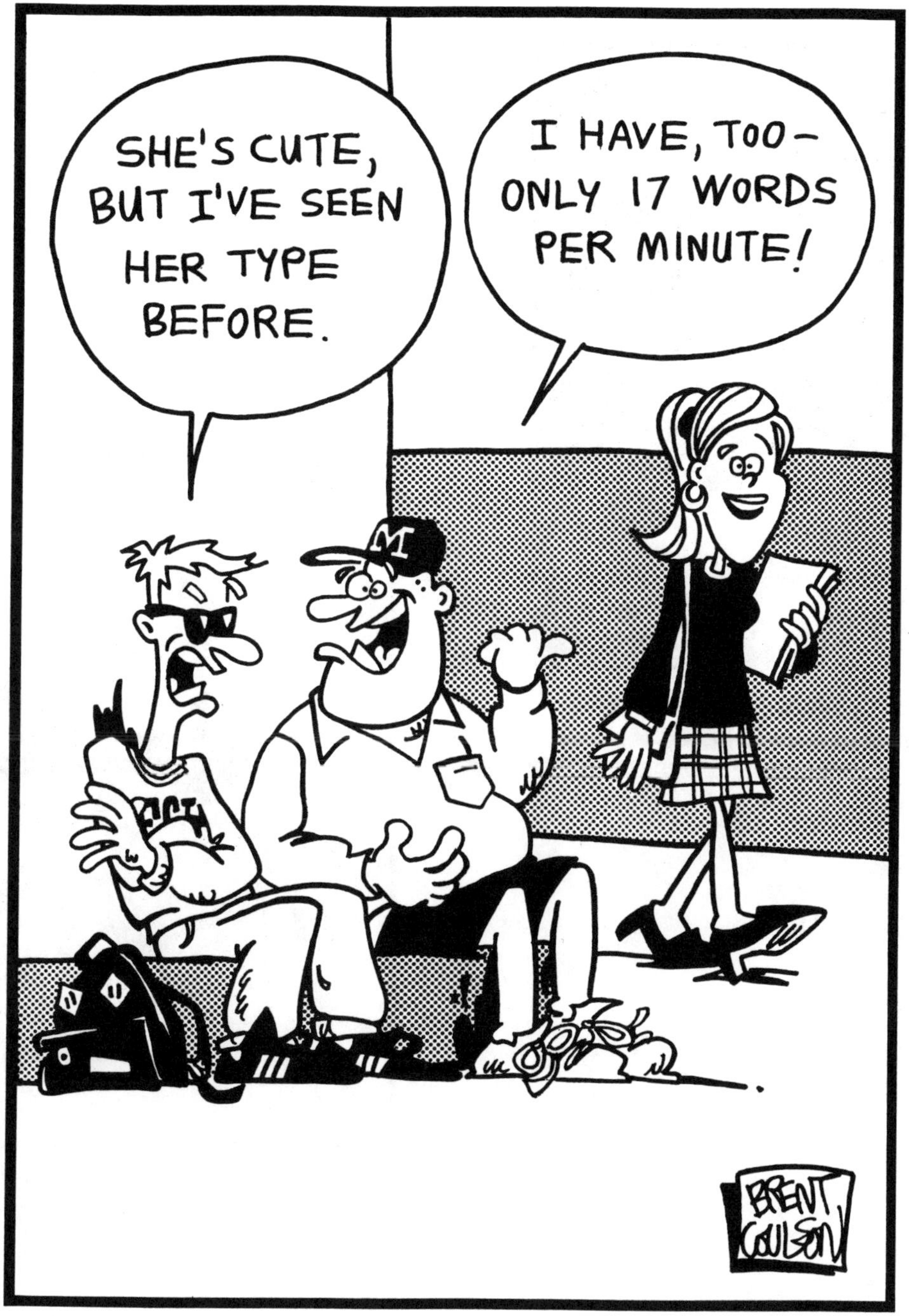
SHE'S CUTE, BUT I'VE SEEN HER TYPE BEFORE.
I HAVE, TOO—ONLY 17 WORDS PER MINUTE!
BRENT COULSON

"And close that door! Where were you raised — in a barn?"

Knights in White Satin

**Mrs. Picasso's refrigerator showed how young
Pablo's style was already developing.**

"Well detective, this is where we found
the dead body of the contortionist..."

Although he could not see his reflection, Dracula was still very self-conscious when he lost his first fang at age six.

Through a stroke of luck, Rex found the vet's phone number in the desk drawer.

Thomas Edison invents the light bulb

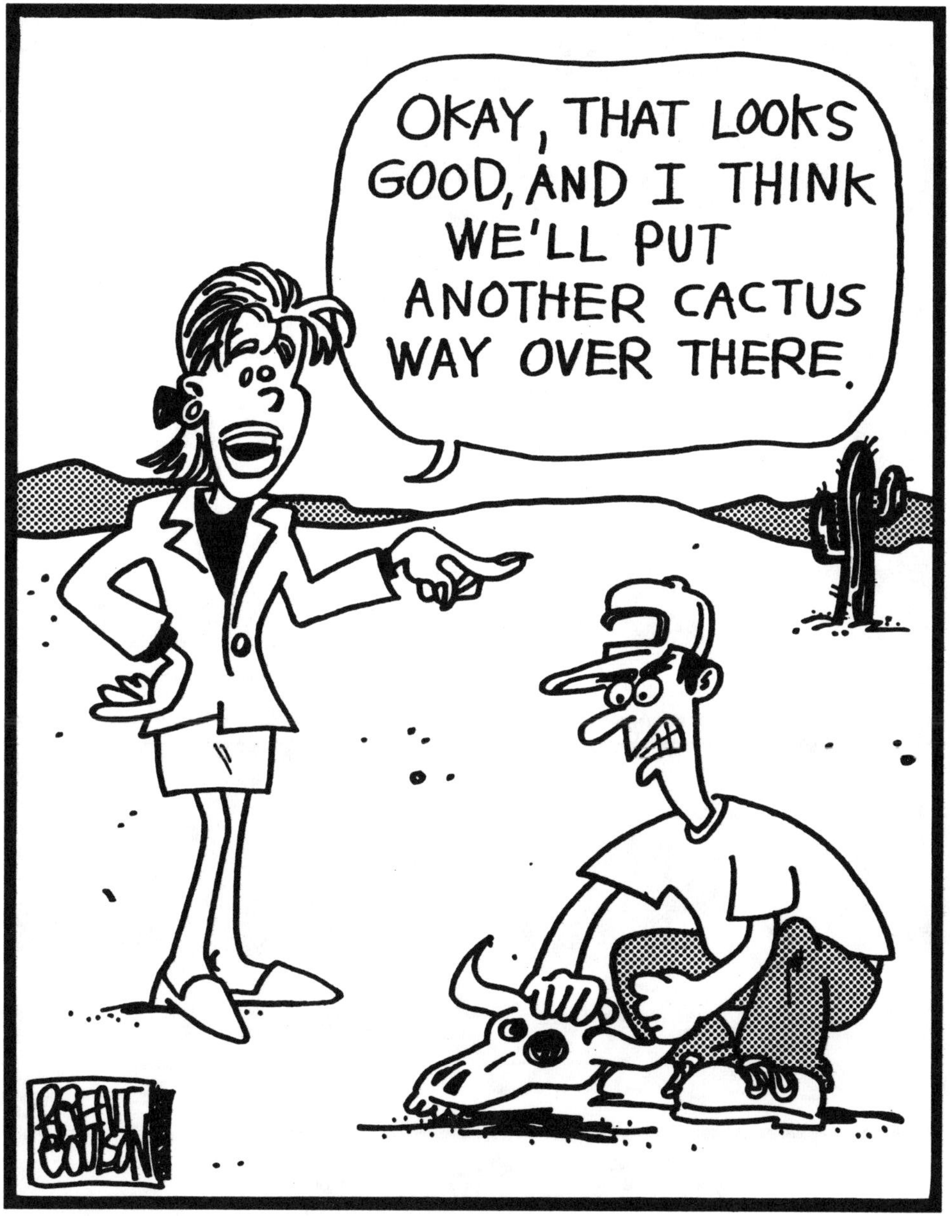
OKAY, THAT LOOKS GOOD, AND I THINK WE'LL PUT ANOTHER CACTUS WAY OVER THERE.

Desert decorators

"Hey Carl, it looks like we
hit the jackpot!"

"Uh-oh Ernie, it says here we were supposed to put the worms on the hooks *before* we put the lines in the water!"

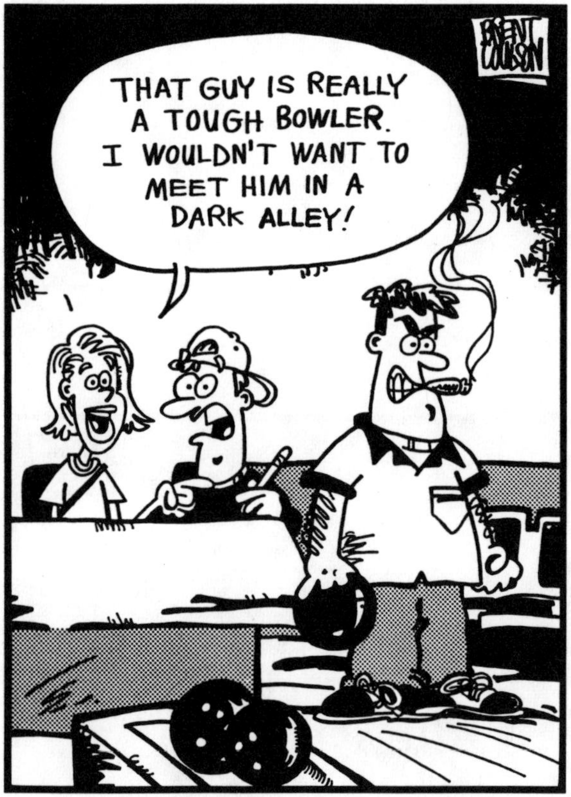
BRENT COULSON
THAT GUY IS REALLY A TOUGH BOWLER. I WOULDN'T WANT TO MEET HIM IN A DARK ALLEY!

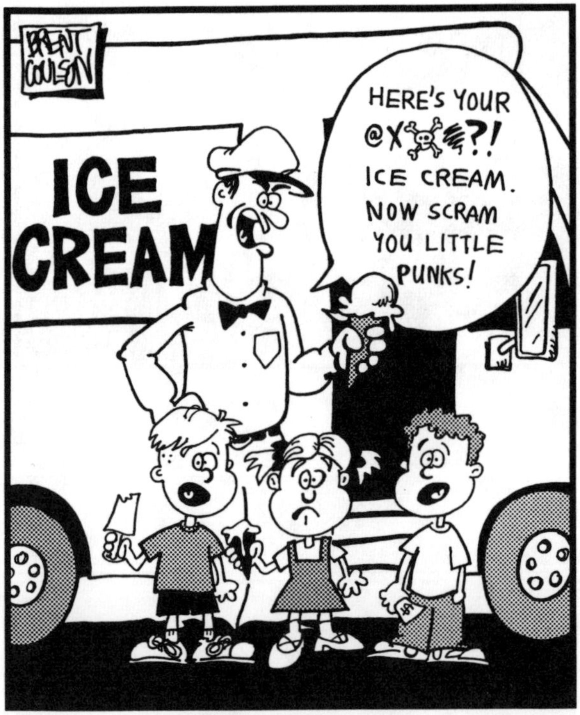
BRENT COULSON
ICE CREAM
HERE'S YOUR @X ?! ICE CREAM. NOW SCRAM YOU LITTLE PUNKS!

The Bad Humor Man

"Hello Mr. Shifflett, I understand that you're here to have a mole removed..."

To his dismay, Tarzan discovered that he had grabbed a bungee cord instead of a vine.

"Well Elliot, it looks like you're out. Simon didn't say 'Draw!'"

The United States Navel Observatory

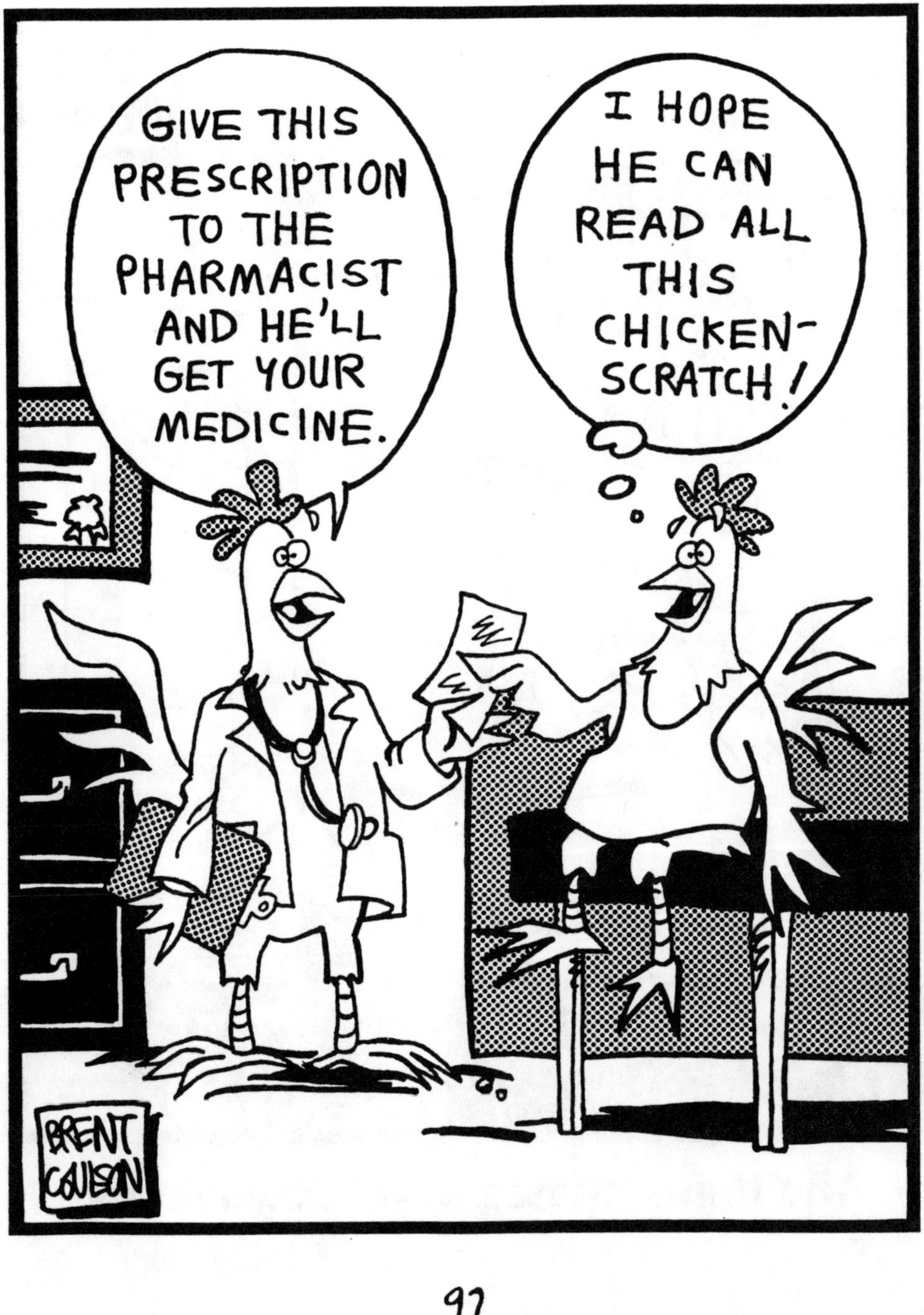
GIVE THIS PRESCRIPTION TO THE PHARMACIST AND HE'LL GET YOUR MEDICINE.
I HOPE HE CAN READ ALL THIS CHICKEN-SCRATCH!
BRENT COULSON

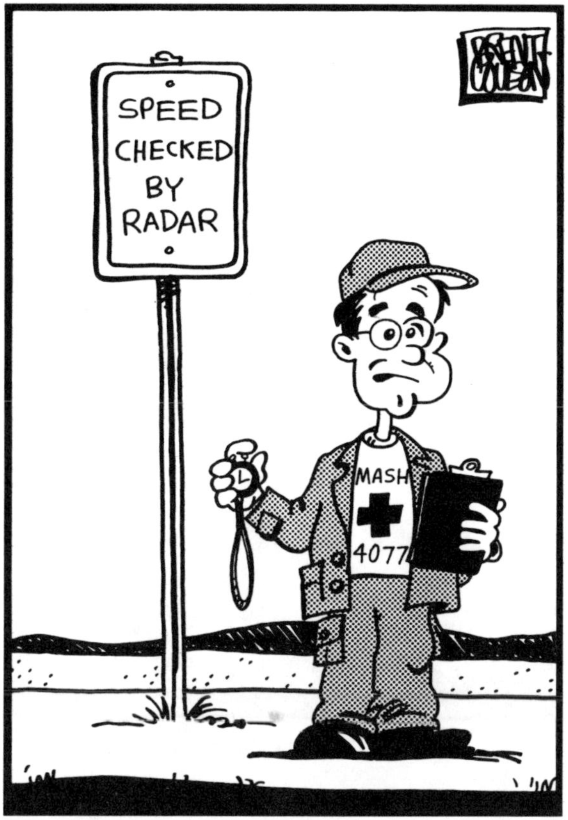
BRENT COULSON
SPEED CHECKED BY RADAR
MASH
4077

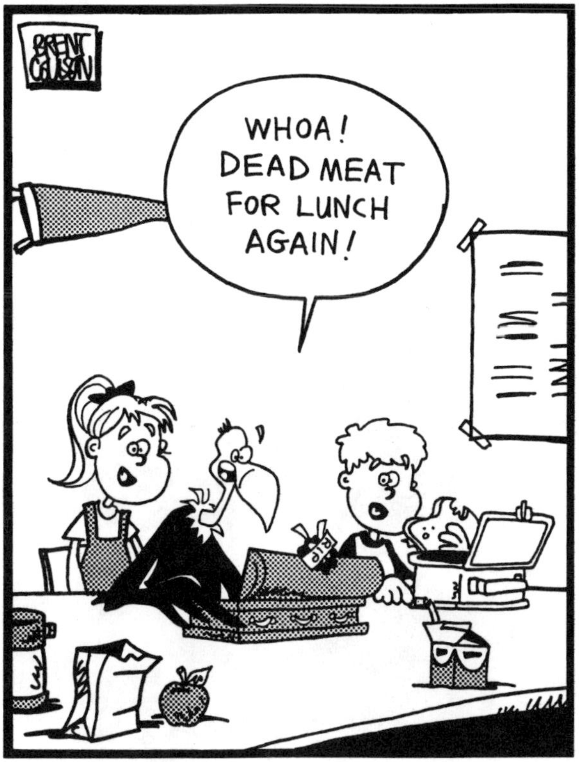
BRENT COULSON
WHOA! DEAD MEAT FOR LUNCH AGAIN!
RIP

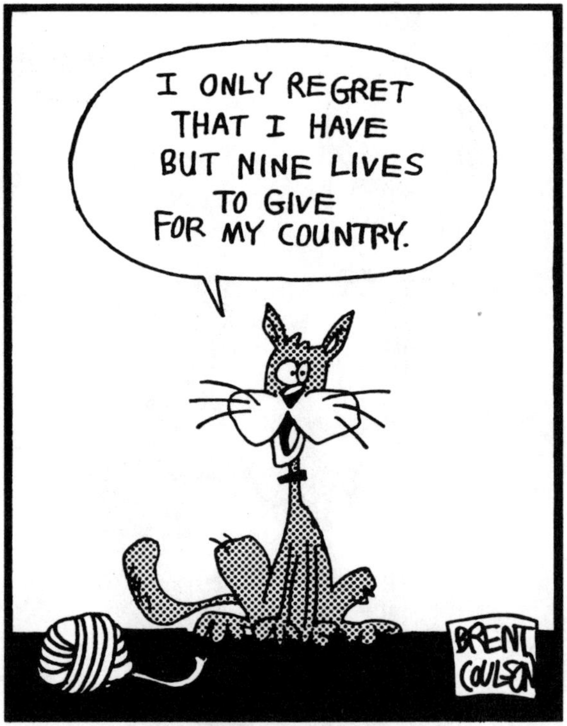
I ONLY REGRET THAT I HAVE BUT NINE LIVES TO GIVE FOR MY COUNTRY.
BRENT COULSON

Nathan Hale's cat

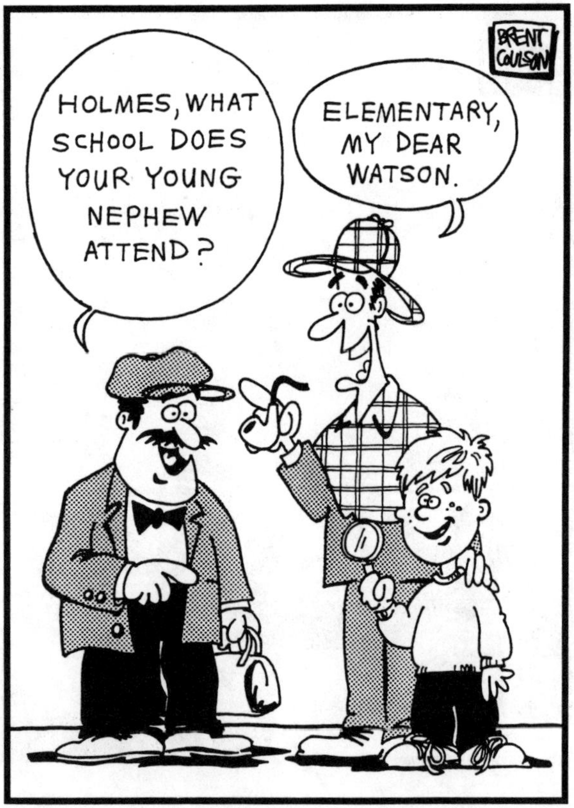
BRENT COULSON
HOLMES, WHAT SCHOOL DOES YOUR YOUNG NEPHEW ATTEND?
ELEMENTARY, MY DEAR WATSON.

Miniature golf caddies

**"Oh, I thought you said they were *cannonballs!*
This is a whole different story!"**

96

"Is this *the key* to the restroom, or is this the restroom *itself*?"

Cyclops in Little League

"It's from Kevin. He sent us a gift certificate but he crossed out the amount so we wouldn't know how much he spent."

"Your honor, the defendant has no alibi, his fingerprints were found on the murder weapon, and let's just face it, *he's a killer bee!*"

Larry rubbed and rubbed, but he couldn't get a genie to come out of the lamp.

Michelangelo, as a disgruntled teen, spray-painted the bathroom of the Sistine Chapel.

"Well, it's not exactly 'Hell on Wheels,'
if that's what you're looking for."

"...and on that farm he had
some cheerleaders..."

Where toilet paper tubes come from

"You are so stupid you'd probably forget
your head if I hadn't attached it!"

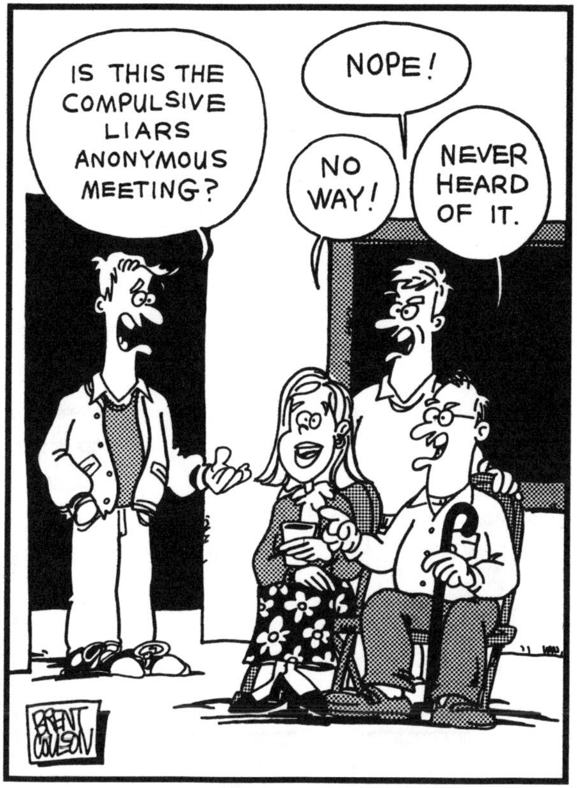
IS THIS THE COMPULSIVE LIARS ANONYMOUS MEETING?
NOPE!
NO WAY!
NEVER HEARD OF IT.
BRENT COULSON

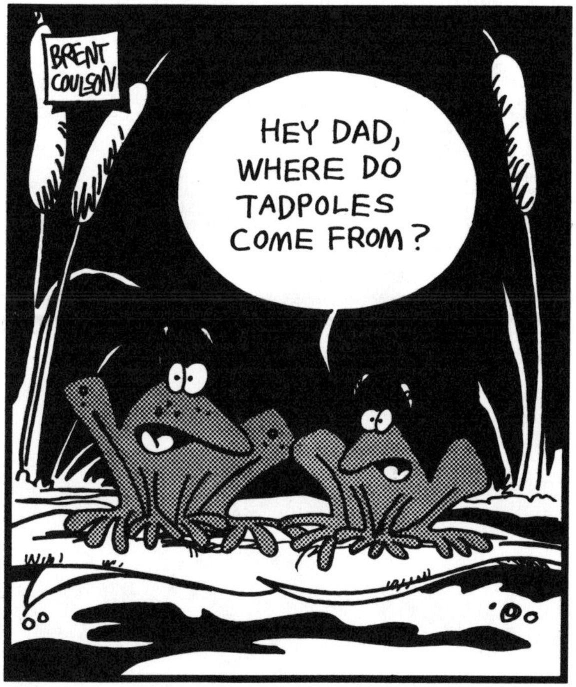
BRENT COULSON
HEY DAD, WHERE DO TADPOLES COME FROM?

Dog catchers

"Hey Dad, are you sure the cat knows what she's supposed to do in the litterbox?"

Restaurants before there was fire

107

As they grew older, the Dukes of Hazzard had much more trouble climbing into their car.

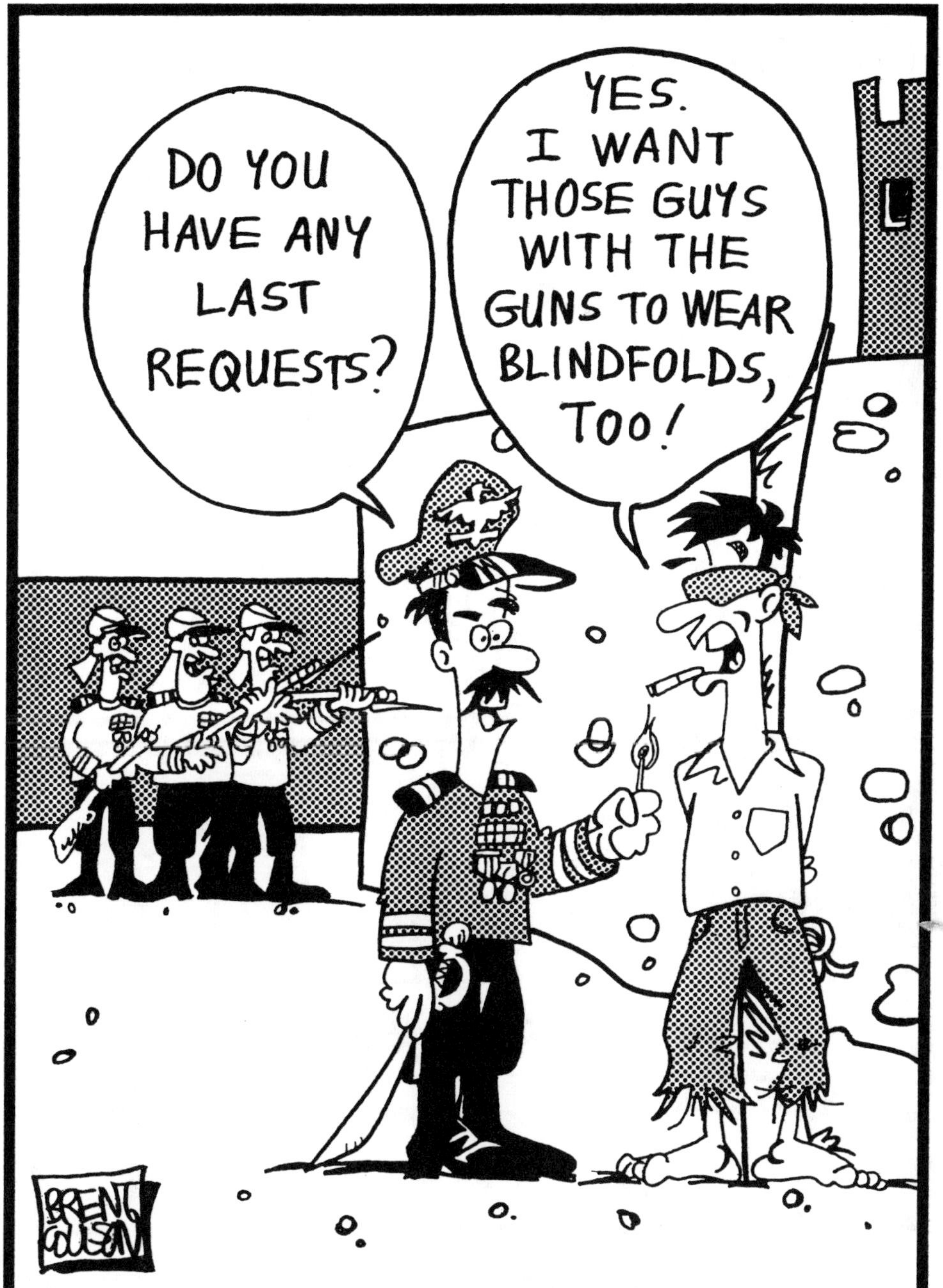
DO YOU HAVE ANY LAST REQUESTS?
YES. I WANT THOSE GUYS WITH THE GUNS TO WEAR BLINDFOLDS, TOO!
BRENT COULSON

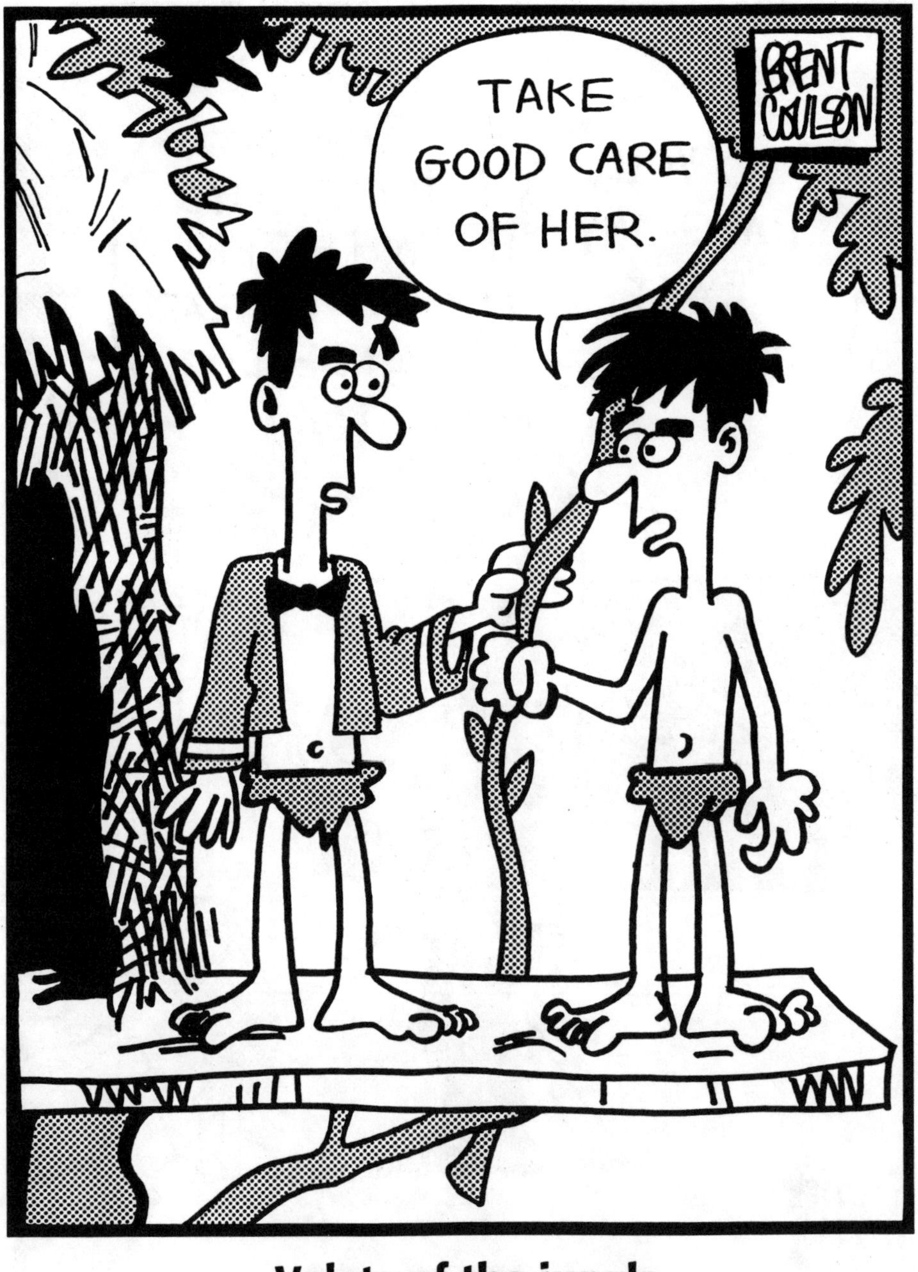
TAKE GOOD CARE OF HER.
BRENT COULSON

Valets of the jungle

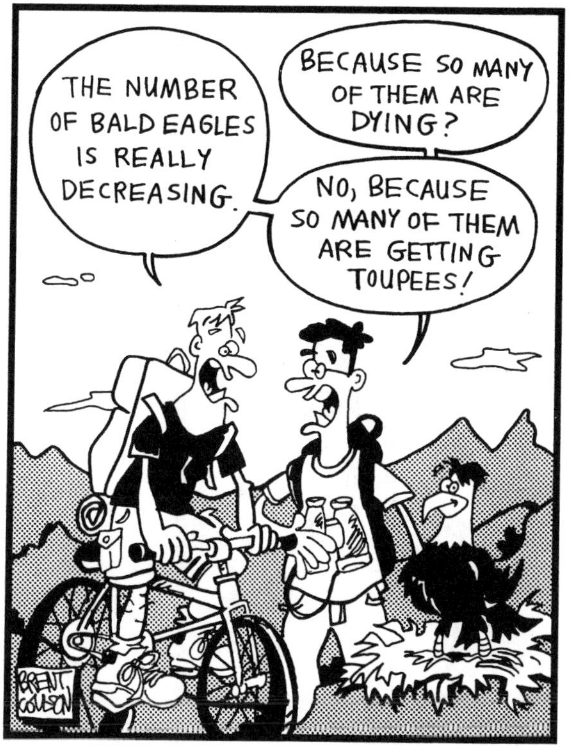
THE NUMBER OF BALD EAGLES IS REALLY DECREASING.
BECAUSE SO MANY OF THEM ARE DYING?
NO, BECAUSE SO MANY OF THEM ARE GETTING TOUPEES!
BRENT COULSON

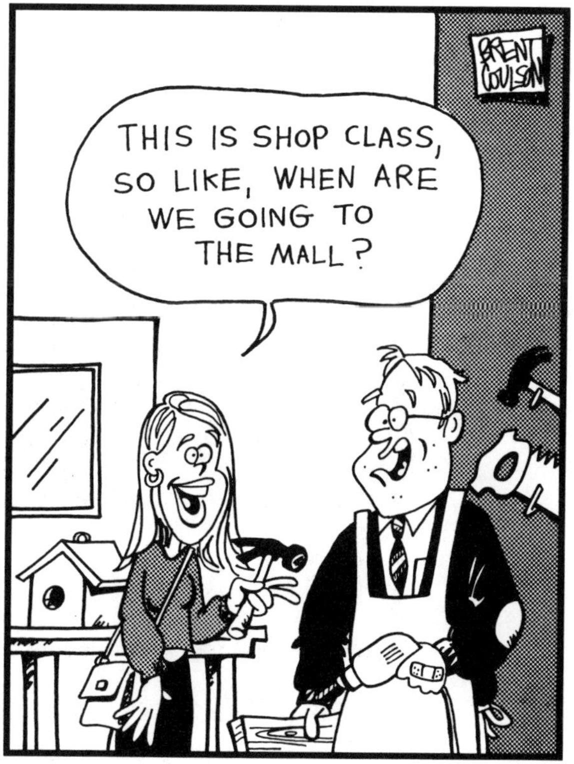
BRENT COULSON
THIS IS SHOP CLASS, SO LIKE, WHEN ARE WE GOING TO THE MALL?

**The shirt said "One size fits all,"
but they all had a tough time
squeezing into it.**